British Toby Jugs

by

Vic Schuler

Edited by F J Salmon and K J Pearson

Published in the United Kingdom by
Kevin Francis Publishing Limited
Landcroft House, 85 Landcroft Rd
East Dulwich, London SE22 9JS

Typeset by SDM Typesetting Ltd, and printed in England by
The Greenwich Press, London SE7.

To my wife Peggy who for years has threatened me with a divorce "if one more Toby comes into the house". I thus have the added pleasure, not only of 'the hunt' for a new find, but also of smuggling it into my collection!

Acknowledgments

I wish to thank Pat Halfpenny and Arnold Mountford of the Stoke-on-Trent museum for making corrections and suggestions, and I would also like to thank the following:

Elizabeth Caper and Tony Wood of Tony Wood (Studio) 82 Ltd. Fenton
Jocelyn Lukins
Dora Shaw of Wood and Sons, Burslem
Joan Jones of the Minton museum, Stoke-on-Trent
Christies of South Kensington & King Street, London
W. F. Greenwood & Sons of Harrogate
Phillips of London
Sotheby's of London & Chester
Wintertons of Lichfield
Diane and Ray Ginns
David (Elias Clark) Antiques
John Gould of the Gladstone Museum
Mr Bailey of Blakeney Art Pottery

Also for information and help with my collection over the years: Percy Chapman, Justin Garrard, Jonathan Horne, Eric Hudes, Terry Ledwith, Leonard Russell, Ronald A. Smith, Vera & Syd Wright, and Jennifer Shaw & Tracy Still for their typing of the original manuscript. Also, Frank Broughton, Jim Challenger and Julie McWilliams.

I wish to thank in particular my editors, Kevin Pearson and Francis Salmon for so much time spent editing and sorting out what had become a jumble of notes when additions to the original manuscript were made and finally, but not least, my wife for being so tolerant, if not always understanding.

First Edition
Kevin Francis Publishing Ltd. Landcroft House, 85 Landcroft Rd, East Dulwich, London SE22 9JS

ISBN 0951076825

Note on Valuations Given in this Book

Within the contents of this book the reader will find valuations of particular jugs, these must only be used as a reference point and not as a hard and fast value of a particular jug. They are included here because so many readers, whether collectors or not, are likely to have a jug which they find very difficult to identify in terms of age, maker or character, and some record as to value may be of help if this book is to fulfill its function.

Auction prices have been recorded where appropriate, but so many jugs do not appear at auctions, and where this is the case, some tentative suggestions have been made to indicate the value of the jug in question. Some jugs are likely to be worth very little whilst others can be worth thousands, but the true value of a jug is the price which someone is willing and able to pay for it, so unless there is a buyer the prices given cannot fulfil their promise.

The reader might also take into account that at auction, premiums and taxes have to be paid on the price a jug makes under the hammer, and dealers will also have to make something of a profit from the work they do in selling the jug. The simple function of the values given is to indicate the value of a jug to a collector, not the asking price to a dealer.

Of course the condition of a jug makes a vast amount of difference to its value. Many have been restored, and it is the extent of restoration which is most important. If the Toby is extremely rare then even a substantial amount of restoration may not detract too much from its value, but if the jug is quite common even a crack may reduce its value quite considerably.

About the Author

Vic Schuler was born in 1918 at Bad-Shot-Lea, Surrey, and spent most of his early boyhood in Surrey and Sussex with his grandparents, his grand-father being a downland Shepherd. He moved to his parents home in London in 1926, and married in 1946.

For fifty years Vic was a tool and die maker, retiring in 1982, but his main interest throughout his life has been British history and antiques. His major obsession, not surprisingly, has been the Toby Jugs which he has collected for the past 25 years.

Throughout the twenties and thirties he took up an avid interest in blues and jazz, collecting many records and pursuing this interest to the ultimate, moving to America from 1948 to 1950 and meeting many of the great pioneer jazz musicians.

On returning to England, his new obsession became English windmills, and he travelled the country in search of these for many years with his wife, Peggy.

From the early sixties to the present day he has had a Saturday stall at the London Portobello Road market and still runs it today, unmistakable in his 'Toby' tricorn hat, selling general antiques, bric-a-brac, and, of course, Tobies.

Vic Schuler is a confessed romantic who likes nothing modern and thinks we are living in an age of ugly buildings, slovenly clothes and tasteless music. In spite of growing up through the depressions of the twenties and thirties, he would not have missed a moment of it!

Contents

Ralph Wood Toby c1795

Chapter One

The reader will initially be concerned with the origin of the Toby Jug and may expect some definitive answers as to why the Toby Jug came about and who first made the character in its original form, but tracing the early life of the Toby is not easy, as will become apparent throughout this book.

In assessing the age of a jug and its maker, the collector must learn something of 'the feel', the texture, the colours used in glazing and the weight and style of potting, rather than rely on makers marks on the bottom of the jug. The collector must develop his own skills of judgement, and it is these individual skills which spice the debate as to the age of jugs, their maker and their value.

Who was Toby?

There are a number of suggestions as to which character inspired the production of the first 'Toby'.

In the eighteenth century the profession of the 'Foot-pad' was known as the 'Low Toby'. He was today's equivalent of the street mugger, and he was obviously not very well liked. The more romanticised figure of the same ilk is the Highwayman on horse-back, who was known as the 'High Toby'. While this is worth a mention it is unlikely that there is an association here with the character as we know him.

Some also see him as the Shakespearian character of the same name in 'Twelfth Night'. Certainly the character is a drinking, foolhardy man, but a more viable claim is that he was one of two notorious drinkers of the late eighteenth century who were reputed to have drunk a great deal of 'Stingo', a strong British ale of the time. One such was Henry Elwes, a Yorkshireman, who died in 1761 having drunk an estimated 2,000 gallons of the beer from a brown jug and was nicknamed 'Toby Fillpot'. The other claim is accorded to Paul Parnel who was acknowledged for his drinking prowess in 'Gentleman's Magazine' of 1810 for drinking "out of one silver cup upwards of £9,000 sterling worth of Yorkshire Stingo, being remarkably attached to Stingo tipple of the homebrewed best quality". At less than one pence per pint in today's terms, this was really going some, but whatever the modesty of the Yorkshire drinker in assessing the drinking prowess of his fellow

Dighton print, 1761 of Toby Fillpot. Courtesy of the British Museum

man, we must at least consider the statistical accuracy of information gathered whilst 'under the influence'.

More convincing evidence as to the origins of the Toby Jug is found in the popularity of a mezzotint produced by Robert Dighton to accompany a song written in 1761 by the Rev. Francis Faulks — a humorous and very British adaptation of the Latin poem by Geranimo Amelto.

This song is presumably to be sung holding a pot of foaming ale, whilst the singer explains how the jug which he holds is made from the deceased body of Toby Fillpot, or 'Phillpot':

The Brown Jug

Dear Tom, this brown jug that now foams with mild ale
(In which I will drink to sweet Nan of the Vale),
Was once Toby Fillpot, a thirsty old soul,
As e're drank a bottle or fathom'd a bowl;
In boozing about 'twas his praise to excel,
And among jolly Toppers he bore off the bell.

It chanced as in dog-days he sat at his ease
In his flow'r-woven arbour as gay as you please,
With a friend and a pipe puffing sorrows away
And with honest old stingo was soaking his clay
His breath doors of life on a sudden were shut
And he died full as big as a Dorchester butt.

His body, when long in the ground it had lain,
And time into clay had resolved it again,
A potter found out in its covert so smug,
And with part of fat Toby he form'd this brown jug
Now sacred to friendship, and mirth, and mild ale,
So here's to my lovely sweet Nan of the Vale.
Courtesy of the British Museum

The song thus gives us both the drinking man and the character. It is known that this print was very popular towards the end of the eighteenth century, such prints being a means of passing on information in the more primitive form of media presentation than that which we know today. Aside from characterising popularly known figures of the day, fictional characters representing the mood of the time (like John Bull and Toby Fillpot) were also developed and incorporated into British life and culture by this means of communication.

This print was originally copied as 'sprigging' (a moulded decoration applied to the sides of various types of pottery) for brown

Toby in under and over glaze colours c1810 drinking Stingo

A Twyford Toby Jug with a cream coloured glaze mottled with splashes of green. Made c1780, it is worth more than £750 in spite of restoration. Courtesy of Sothebys.

salt-glazed stoneware, sometimes also referred to as 'Toby Jugs'. This sprigging has been used by various potters including Doulton in the nineteenth century. The decoration has also been used for plaques and is found on Pratt-ware jugs such as those marked 'Ferrybridge'. John Turner is thought to have produced the first mould of this print, a faithful representation, a copy of which can be seen in the museum at Spode's Pottery, Stoke-on-Trent.

From the song we can ascertain that the date, the style of clothes, the jug and the pipe are just about right to form a model for the first traditional Toby Jug.

A point worth mentioning here is that jugs in the human form have been produced ever since man began making pottery, the Greeks and Romans also producing them, but the peculiarity of the British Toby Jug is in its resemblance to the Toby of the print, in drinking pose. The reason for the Toby Jug becoming so named is that 'Toby' is referred to in the third line of the song, thus giving an appropriate name for this particular type of jug.

What were Toby Jugs used for?

It has been claimed that Toby Jugs were used to convey ale to tables in country taverns. The ordinary nine to ten inch Toby is quite large and would hold about a quart of ale, but in fact, whilst they may be an adaptation of the ordinary jugs of a similar size and shape, it is unlikely that they were ever viewed as being practical. They are probably no more than ornamental vessels, fulfilling all the prerequisites of an ordinary jug, even being made with a detachable hat-crown which could possibly have been used to protect the contents from the 'smuts' created by tallow candles used for lighting purposes at the time. It is more plausibly suggested that these hats could have been used for drinking from.

The original Toby Jug was possibly big enough to carry ale, but subsequent jugs, made towards the end of the eighteenth century and thereafter, such as the 'Hearty Good Fellow', were totally inappropriate for carrying any liquid, the neck being far too small to pour from, and the inside of the jugs being particularly difficult to clean. This hygiene aspect was all the more important in the mid-nineteenth century when cleanliness was realised to be a prime factor in the fight against the spread of disease. So much so, in fact, that pottery cow creamer jugs fell out of favour during the Great Cholera Epidemic of the 1850s. The Toby survived because it is unlikely that it was in use as a jug.

Although the original Toby Jug may have served some practical purpose initially it can generally be taken that its function was subsequently nothing more than ornamental.

Chapter Two
Who made the first Toby Jug? The early makers

Just who made the first Toby Jug is really a matter of conjecture. There were many potters in the Staffordshire potteries who in the last quarter of the eighteenth century could have produced the first Toby.

The three most commonly cited potters of the early jugs are **John Astbury of Shelton (1688-1743)**, **Thomas Whieldon of Fenton (1719-1795)** and **Ralph Wood I of Burslem (1715-1772)**, but there is no evidence that any of them made the first standard Toby Jug. It is important that we look briefly at why these potters could or could not have produced the first jugs before going on to look at the arguments for **John Wood, Ralph Wood II** and some other early potters as being among the first of the makers of the British Toby Jug which is so familiar to us all today.

We can establish the fact that the first potters of the British Toby Jug lived within the small area known as the Staffordshire Potteries. Identification of who did what in the eighteenth century is virtually impossible, not only because potters did not mark their work, but also because in the narrow confines of the area in which they lived, potters often worked with one another and for one another, so it is difficult to distinguish between them. Indeed the potteries of that period can be seen as one interrelated family — they married one another's sisters, they pilfered one another's ideas, they went into business with one another, they lent money and gave credit to one another — in fact they almost lived and worked as a single family, with all the quarrelling, feuding and imitating reminiscent of today's popular soap operas.

Toby Jugs which sell under the name of **Astbury** are most unlikely to be his, although the jugs known as the 'Fiddler and Midshipmite Group' ascribed to him are the most sought after of all Tobies. They are certainly early, but the type of pottery, modelling and glazing differ from what we might expect of Astbury. They are primitive in their style of potting, with some of the Astbury look about them, but no shards (broken pieces of pottery) were found at the excavation site of his pottery in Shelton which could justify the claim that he made Toby Jugs. They were probably made after his death by some unknown potter and they are unlikely to be the jugs which inspired continued production for the next two hundred years. Only one of this group of jugs is a drinking Toby in something of the form which we know today.

Whieldon-type step Toby. Made c1770

Whieldon-type Toby c1780

Fiddler Toby c1770, Astbury type

Neale & Co 'Ordinary' Toby c1795, marked on base, courtesy of G A Godden.

Ralph Wood mould no 51. Made c1790. Courtesy of the Stoke on Trent Museum

Similar problems arise with **'Whieldon'** jugs which can bring large sums at auction. These jugs are again quite primitively produced, but once more, there is no documentary evidence to substantiate Whieldon's status as an early potter of Toby Jugs. He never marked his wares and again, there are no broken shards at the evacuation site of his pottery in Fenton which might indicate that he was producing them. These jugs do not look quite as primitive as the so called Astbury-type, and must be termed Whieldon-type if anything, though sometimes they are cited as being by Twyford. They can be identified by their mottled decoration and, quite often, by a relatively small jug held in Toby's hand which has a distinctive pear-shape. Other criteria for regarding a Toby as Whieldon is a step-base (referred to in detail later) and black staring eyes which can give the Toby a rather frightening appearance. It is quite possible that these jugs were being produced from c.1765, but we shall never know who produced them, or exactly when.

It seems that there is some confusion as to the potting status of Astbury and Whieldon. Their names are often used generically, in association with the types of potting practice for which they are famous rather than in the context of their being the definite producers of particular types of pottery. So it is quite inaccurate to term all eighteenth century Tobies with running mottled glazes as 'Whieldon' or those with the primitively styled modelling of the Fiddler and Midshipmite type as 'Astbury'.

The greatest misnomer relating to the popularly held conceptions of the early producers of Toby Jugs relates to **Ralph Wood I**, who is considered to have produced among the finest examples of the British Toby in a fashion which has laid the standard for all the other potters of the last two centuries. Whilst it is true that these Tobies are among the best made in the eighteenth century and they do seem to follow the theme of Toby Fillpot of the song referred to previously, Ralph Wood I can no longer, on current evidence, be regarded as the maker of these jugs. He worked for the Wedgwoods for the bulk of his career, certainly the last fourteen years, and achieved only the status of a block cutter, signing his name on the saltglazed stoneware blocks which were used for making moulds. There is certainly no record of any pot-bank where Ralph Wood I could have produced figures and Toby Jugs at any time during his life.

The confusion stems largely from the fact that 'R WOOD' and 'Ra Wood Burslem' appear on a number of late eighteenth century figures (and at least one Toby), and this is taken to be Ralph Wood I or his son of the same name, Ralph Wood II. Thus it has been thought that both men produced a range of high quality figures and Toby Jugs between them. It has also been thought that Ralph Wood I was responsible for the jugs which have running coloured glazes, an unglazed base, and the impressed name, 'R WOOD', whilst his son used fixed enamel glazes, glazed the base of his jugs and impressed his name 'Ra Wood Burslem'. But this simply cannot be true, the different methods of glazing were in use concurrently towards the end of the eighteenth century and Ralph Wood I could not really have produced his own Tobies and figures. We cannot therefore make the same distinction between father and son which has been popular in the past.[1]

In fact, even Ralph Wood II is unlikely to have made a significant number of the figures and Toby Jugs popularly held to be his. He spent a number of years away from Burslem, in Bristol, (from 1774 to 1783) selling earthenware and glass, and when he did return he worked with Enoch Wood, his cousin, until around 1789. Only from then to his death in 1795 did he produce his own wares in his own pot-bank.

As if this confusion over the Ralph Woods were not enough, we have also to contend with the fact that Ralph Wood III took over his father's pot-bank from 1795 to 1801 until his death at the early age of twenty-six. The only certainty over any of the Tobies attributed to the Ralph Woods is the one that bears the mould number '51' and the impressed mark 'R Wood Burslem' on the base. On current evidence this is likely to have been made between 1789 and 1801, by either Ralph Wood II or Ralph Wood III.

One other source relating to the Ralph Woods is the oft quoted invoice from Ralph Wood II to Thomas and John Wedgwood in 1783. This is for a group of figures (there are no Toby Jugs on the list), and since he had only recently returned from Bristol it must be that he was either selling his old stock or acting on behalf of his brother, John Wood.

It seems that it was **John Wood Snr (1743-1797)**, the brother of Ralph Wood II who not only produced many of the major figures thought to be by Ralph Wood I and II, but also many of the Toby Jugs. He has been much neglected as a result of the fact that he did not mark his work, but he was a successful potter from around 1775 onwards and is known to have sold Toby Jugs in the year 1786 to a Mr John Edwards — four Toby Jugs 'coloured' for ten shillings and two 'china glaze' for four shillings. It is quite likely that he made Tobies before this date and he certainly has the most significant claim to producing the first of the standard British Tobies and variations on the theme, because he is known to have produced Tobies in the 1780s and we also know that he was reasonably successful — something which cannot be said of the Ralph Woods.

Because of the evidence that both men produced Toby Jugs, John Wood and Ralph Wood must share the honours for being the producers of erstwhile 'Ralph Wood Tobies', setting the standards for future

[1]Much of the information in this section comes from Pat Halfpenny's 'The Wood Family' in Ceramics III 1986.

Portobello Toby c1840. Courtesy of D & R Ginns

Overglaze Toby probably by John Walton c1820

Two Pratt type Jugs c1800. Courtesy of D & R Ginns

Pratt type c1800. 8″ high.

Marked Davenport with anchor and dated 1836

Yorkshire Toby c1800

Pratt with dark brown face. Could be called a Negro or Collier, except hands are white

potters, even though they may not have been the first. It may be better, therefore, to refer to those jugs with the Wood features as 'Wood-type' rather than as 'Ralph Wood'.

The origin of the following Tobies has previously been accredited to Ralph Wood, but we must also include John Wood as a possible maker.

The Ordinary

The Ordinary with right hand holding beaker (mould no 51)

The Long-faced Ordinary

The Sharp-faced Ordinary

The Roman-nose Ordinary

Martha Gunn

Lord Howe or Man on a Barrel (mould no 63)

Prince Hal

The Sailor (mould no 65)

The Squire

The Shield Toby

The Tipsy Man

Mould numbers are known to have been used by the Woods, but they could also have been used by other potters. The three numbers, 51, 63 and 65 are commonly accepted as being mould numbers for Wood jugs, so the collector who finds similar numbers, about ¼″ high impressed in the base of an early jug must ascertain from its quality whether he or she has found a Wood jug. The numbers appear only occasionally.

The work of John and Ralph Wood II is so outstanding that the features which are common to them are unmistakable to the initiated. The fine modelling, the gaping unpainted mouth, the crow's feet at the sides of the eyes, and the general facial expression all have the same hint of quality about them, and once this is recognised by the collector, he should have no difficulty in picking one out from many, saying 'That's an early Wood Toby'.

Enoch Wood was the cousin of John and Ralph Wood, joining forces as a potter with Ralph Wood when Ralph returned to Burslem from Bristol in 1783 and then forming a partnership with James Caldwell in 1790. Enoch Wood is well known for his work in the late eighteenth century, and was known at the time as 'The Father of the Potteries'. It is likely that he too made the conventional Toby and it is often felt that he produced the first versions of the 'George Whitfield' (often called 'The Nightwatchman') and 'The Drunken Parson'.

Palmer, Wilson and **Neale** are also known to be early potters of the Toby Jug and their jugs are of a very good quality, with 'Neale & Co' sometimes being found on the base. Neale was a London supplier of fine pottery who had much of his products made in Staffordshire, only of the best quality. Some of his Tobies are so similar to those taken to be by the Woods that they could easily be mistaken as such, though some marked ones are not of such high quality.

Toby Jugs by different potters can be so similar that it is worth noting here some of the reasons for this. One reason is that the skilled modellers who worked at the potteries were a rare commodity and worked for different potters on a self employed basis, sometimes only for a number of days. It is not unreasonable to suppose that the modeller of the Wood-type Toby Jug may have taken his skills to a rival pottery who then produced something very similar. Another reason for a very great similarity between the work of different potters, not only in the eighteenth century but on to the present day, is that potters often used one another's moulds, buying and selling bankrupt stock, and so *the same* Toby may have been produced by more than one potter. After all, we must remember that the life-span of the average pottery in the Staffordshire area during the eighteenth century was only a very few years and moulds were often sold.

Many other potteries, at the time and since, have caught up on the popularity of the Toby Jug, producing their own in many different variations. **Pratt-type** jugs of this early period were made in quite large numbers. Pratt-type decoration can be noted for its distinctive colouring, with yellows, blues and browns showing up brightly against a grey-blue earthenware. The most common feature of this type of decoration is the spotted pattern on many of the pieces, but it is unlikely that they were all made at the same pottery, the Pratt name being used generically.

We must not delude ourselves that all early Toby Jug production has came from Staffordshire. Many other potteries throughout Britain, like the **Swansea** pottery in Wales, made fine Toby Jugs and its wares were usually marked from c1780-1824. **Portobello** near Edinburgh, Scotland, made Tobies which can be identified by its use of a bright maroon enamel colour (from c1840) and the **Yorkshire** area was also a prolific producer of Toby Jugs in the late eighteenth century and the first half of the nineteenth century (esp. **Leeds**).

Among the most common of the Tobies made in the traditional way are those by **Davenport**. He closely followed the eighteenth century craftsmen both in technique and general characteristics, and thus deserves mention, but he produced well into the nineteenth century and allowed himself to be influenced by prevailing fashions, turning his talents to the production of brilliantly enamelled pottery and heavy gilding, far below the standards set by the Woods.

John **Walton** is another of these early potters who were producing

Tobies in the eighteenth century, but he too is largely considered to be a nineteenth century potter. Although his wares were made for the lower classes and were mass produced in order to meet the limits of their purse, they were the best of their kind and had a certain originality about them. These jugs can sometimes be found with 'Walton' impressed on a raised ribbon under the base or on the back of the jug.

The excessive use of gilt and garish colours as well as the loss of modelling definition in favour of mass production techniques sets in from around 1840. There was a rapid deterioration in all artistic taste in England from the beginning of Queen Victoria's reign but it must not be taken from this that the later jugs like those of Davenport and Walton are of no value. They are still considered to be collectors items in spite of the deterioration in quality. Generally, though, it is not until the twentieth century that the balance is redressed, with some very fine Toby Jugs being produced.

Inspite of the confusion over who the first makers of Toby Jugs were, we can take it that even if the Woods were not the first potters, they certainly set a standard for other potters to follow up until the present day. At some time in the future we may be able to distinguish between the Woods and decide just who made what, but for the present we must be content to look out for their Tobies and those of other early potters who put so much effort and individuality into every one they produced.

Chapter Three: The Ordinary Toby

Pratt-type Toby c1800

'Ordinary' with head slightly turned to left. c1845

Hollins c1800. 12¼" high

Shorter c1920, 12½" high

This is the most common type of Toby Jug and the one which formed the original blueprint for the Tobies which are still in production today — and which, no doubt, will still be in production a hundred years from now.

The 'Ordinary' Toby is usually 9″-10″ high, depicting a seated figure clothed in eighteenth century style dress, the distinguishing feature being his tricorn hat. In the late eighteenth century this hat was known as a 'Kefenhuller' and it was the standard male headgear throughout Europe and North America. Such hats were not commonly worn by sea captains, nor were they worn by Nelson and Napoleon as many people think (they wore bicorn hats). By and large the original tricorn hat was worn by the ordinary beer drinking man enjoying a pot of ale and a smoke.

The 'Ordinary' Toby figure wears a long top-coat which would fall just below the knees when standing. Under this he wears a waistcoat and has a scarf or 'stock' around his neck. He wears breeches down to the knees and stockings underneath. His shoes are either fastened with buckles or tied with laces. On his left knee he balances a jug of ale which is usually full, and it is held by the left hand whilst the right supports it.

An interesting variation of this would be to find an 'Ordinary' Toby with the jug held in the right hand and balanced on the right knee instead of the other way round. These are rare, and it would be interesting to learn of any — but if you are working from a photograph it is as well to bear in mind that the print may have been reproduced in reverse.

Two potteries made larger than usual figures of the 'Ordinary' Toby. They were **'Hollins of Hanley' 1794-1820** and **'Shorter of Stoke', c.1920-30**. The Hollins Toby is 12¼″ high with a pipe down by the right leg. Shorter made a copy of the same jug without the pipe which is not as attractive as the Hollins jug, being painted in harsh black, brown and yellow colours. The Shorter jug is marked, 'Shorter Made in England'.

Another variation on the 'Ordinary' Toby, which is quite common, is a grey haired Toby, sitting with his head turned very slightly to the left. He can still to be found wearing his detachable hat crown, which has a groove in it running from front to back and a yellow or red band around the hat brim. At the back of the jug is a nicely moulded chair-back and handle. These Tobies were first made around 1840-1850 and continued to be produced into the twentieth century. The earlier versions tend to have softer colours with nice crisp modelling and hollow feet. The later reproductions have the small jug moulded into the body and are sometimes found with '1793' painted on front of base, although they are twentieth century Tobies.

The 'Ordinary' Toby is so common, that it is impossible to give values. One can only say that it is the variations on the 'Ordinary' Toby theme which are most valuable to collectors, and as such the 'Ordinary' tends to fetch slightly less on the market if it has no unusual features. An 'Ordinary' variation by Ralph Wood is the drinking Toby with a glass raised to the mouth, held in the right hand. Because of this distinction *and* the impressed name 'Ra Wood Burslem' with the mould number 51 on the base, this jug fetched £2600 at auction (Sothebys 1986).

There are so many variants of the 'Ordinary' Toby that we must not lose sight of him in the rest of this book. Nearly all the potters who made different characters of the Toby also made the 'Ordinary' Toby which we only briefly mention here. It must be remembered that these variants, the family of which we concentrate on in Chapter 5, spring from the original.

These two jugs display the difference in moulding between the eary jugs and the later Victorian jugs

Wood-type. Note running glaze on hat. Courtesy D & R Ginns

Early 'Ordinary' Toby, smoking pipe

Chapter Four
Identifying the age of a Toby Jug

Identifying the age, quality, character and maker of a jug can be very difficult, and the collector will benefit a great deal from experience, from visiting appropriate museums and antiques shops and reading on the subject. The following indicates the major areas to watch out for on examining and identifying Toby Jugs.

The 'Feel'

A great deal can be learned from the 'feel' of a Toby Jug. Handling them and feeling the weight, warmth and texture of the jug can be very helpful. For instance, some old Tobies which are made of a creamy light body are very thinly potted and are very light in the hand. They can weigh as little as 1lb 11oz, against the weight of the average Toby which is around 2¾lbs.

It is reasonably safe to say that if an ordinary Toby Jug of 9″ to 10″ in height is noticeably light in the hand it will have been produced no later than c1800, as long as it is in keeping with the potting standards of the time. These Tobies are thinly potted earthenware and lack the bulk of clay, warming quickly in the hands. Porcelain and stoneware pottery are always heavier and colder to the touch.

The Glaze

It is also important to look at the glazing. Toby Jugs have been produced in a fascinating array of colours and three different methods of glazing have been used. In fact, unlike much of the mass-produced pottery of today, Toby Jugs of the eighteenth and nineteenth century possess an individuality about them which helps to make them such a fascinating subject for collection. Part of the responsibility for this lies with the artist who initially coloured the jug, much of the painting being very unprofessional, but nonetheless adding a uniqueness to the character. The following shows something about the types of glaze that were used.

Translucent Glaze

Up to c1780, translucent colour glazes were most commonly used for colouring the Toby. These colours were painted on by hand with a brush, but they were quite pale and this may have resulted in small patches on the 'biscuit' being missed. The problem was that after firing, when the glazes revealed their full colours, those omitted patches showed up all the more. This only occurs on translucent glaze jugs, so it is possible to use it as a means of identifying the age of a jug.

The only colours available to the potter for coloured glazes up to 1780 were:

Purple	obtained from manganese
Brown	obtained from manganese and iron
Green	obtained from copper
Blue	obtained from cobalt
Grey	obtained from cobalt
Yellow	obtained from ochre/iron

The shade of the colour was determined by the percentage of oxide used. These colours are beautifully pale and translucent, often running over their intended lines (for example the colour of the hat streaking down the side of the face) but still giving a very pleasing effect. This type of translucent colour glazing is associated with early Wood jugs, sometimes referred to as 'running glaze'.

Underglazing

Using this method the metallic oxides were painted on to the 'biscuit' pottery and a lead glaze applied on top, instead of being mixed with the clear glaze as before. This resulted in a much thicker looking glaze with brighter, harsher colours. It was used from c1780 — c1840 and generally became known as **Pratt type** colours. The 'Pratt' colours are associated with William Pratt of Fenton (1780 — 1799) who used this method of underglaze decoration.

From c1770 cobalt was often added to the glaze, giving a blue welling to the creases in the face, in between the fingers and on clothes etc. This is referred to today as **Pearlware**.

Underglazed Toby c1800

Overglaze

Toby with overglaze colours c1820. This has a 'step base', rare for a jug so late. Note flaking.

This third type of decorating is where the whole palette of colours could be used. The jug was glazed and fired, painted over in enamel colours and fired again at a lower temperature in the 'muffle' oven. The problem with this method was that sometimes the colours tended to peel off, particularly the darker shades, the greatest offender being black. Flaking of colours is a common occurrence and often occurs on Staffordshire pottery. The darker the colour, the greater the risk of flaking; thus for technical reasons black would suffer most.

Colour painting involved firstly giving the biscuit body a clear glaze and firing it. The colour was mixed with a flux and then applied to the clear glaze. This was done by re-firing it at a lower temperature which allowed the glaze to soften sufficiently for the amalgam of colour and flux to fuse with the glaze. However, too much flux caused colour dilution and too little caused poor adhesion which could result in flaking over the years.

In fact it became quite common to use both the underglaze and overglaze methods in conjunction with one another. For example, the collector will often find that where Toby's coat is blue, it is fired in underglaze with the remaining colours in overglaze.

Crazing

Crazing, or 'crackle', occurs when the glaze has contracted from the body of the jug. At first inspection there might not be any crazing visible to the naked eye, but inspection of the jug with an eyeglass will more often than not reveal it. If the crazing is minute, and the area bounded by the craze lines is less than 1/16″ wide, it is an indication of an early jug (prior to c1820). The collector must remember though that crazing can be reproduced quite easily by modern potters.

Jugs with large brown crackle tend to be reproductions in which the crackle has been artifically coloured, usually with coffee stains or the like.

The Face

The colour of Toby's face varies from off-white to black, with jaundice colours, puce and brown between. Some eighteenth century jugs have cheeks which have large patches of manganese or brown on them. These faces often carry warts, pimples and even small pox sores (looking particularly gruesome, showing blood where picked). A black spot appears on the cheek of one eighteenth century Toby in the author's possession and it is interesting to note that William Hogarth used to paint a black spot on the face of some characters in order to denote that he or she had contracted venereal disease!

The undeniable ugliness of some of these Tobies is not an indictment of their collectability; there is something fetching about the truthful representation of an eighteenth century drunken sot who seeks pleasure in beer in order to escape the harsh realities of life. The spots, scabs and 'splodges' are features which add to the necessary ugliness of the jug.

Early Toby showing 'picked' sores on face.

Early Toby with rosy cheeks — a not uncommon feature

In the Georgian period the lips and teeth tended not to be painted in at all because the fine definition in the modelling was thought to be sufficient. The Victorian jugs, being less finely modelled, had lips and teeth emphasised by red paint, giving a far less pleasing effect.

Gilding

During the nineteenth century the gold effect on ceramics was known as 'best gold', which was an amalgam of mercury and gold with a flux. Hence it was also known as 'mercuric gold'. It had a dull appearance and had to be burnished. With the very high cost of gold and the extra labour of hand burnishing, it was expensive. Over the years dusting has often rubbed away the gold, but in 1880, 'bright gold' was introduced. This was in a liquid form and was just brushed on, coming out of the oven bright and finished with no other work to do. The result was that the old 'soft gilt' look was replaced by this new, brassy, harsh look.

This is the gold to be seen on the Allerton Toby Jugs (1859-1942).

Hats/detachable crowns

It seems that all the Toby Jugs of the eighteenth and early nineteenth century were initially made with detachable hat crowns. It is unusual to find them still present now because they were often lost or damaged over time.

Pure black hats are rarely found on early jugs before c1780 and it is interesting to note that on early jugs, the very edge of the brim can go quite yellow, showing that the black appearance is in fact dark brown. A coloured band around the hat brim is found on both eighteenth and nineteenth century jugs.

The Small Jug

A jug of beer is usually held in Toby's hand, with interesting variations in shape, size and decoration. The method of representing the beer froth is worth noting; a single flower appears as froth on the top of some jugs, (which is known to appear quite commonly as knobs on Leeds teapot lids), an all-over pricking effect appears as froth on others, shredded clay (which looks like a pile of worms), or realistically, a bubble effect which is created in the clay. Sometimes this froth flows down the side of the jug.

In the eighteenth century the small jug was not usually decorated, indeed it appears that the Wood-type 'Ordinary' Tobies had no decoration on them and were empty or half full.

Probably Leeds c1790. Note black spot.

Detail of very high quality Toby c1780 showing flower knop as beer froth. Value of this type of Toby around £800.

The small jug must be a separate modelled item and not part of Toby's main body. When the jug in hand forms an integral part of the main body it can be taken as an indication that it was produced after c1840, since such methods were introduced then in order to simplify manufacture with front and back completed in two moulds.

The Handles

Handles have an interesting variation in size, form and decoration. The most spectacular handle on the ordinary Toby is the figurehead type on what is known as the Yorkshire Toby (see page 87). A Wood-type 'Ordinary' model is even known to have a grinning monkey on the top of the handle.

Modelling

Probably the single most important thing to look for on a Toby Jug is good modelling. The modelling should be crisp and vigorous on early jugs, the Toby having well defined teeth, eyelids, facial lines, buttons, buttonholes, and laces. It should also show good definition on the neck scarf and waistcoat.

Hollow Arms and Legs

Many early 'Ordinary' Tobies have hollow feet which overlap the base (some jugs as much as ⅞"). If the feet are hollow, it is safe to say that the jug was produced before c1840. If the Toby is turned upside down, the hollowness of the feet can be detected through the overlap. The feet and legs were always hollow on early jugs, but sometimes a sole was added to the shoes making the hollowness difficult to detect. It may be that the sole-less shoes were necessary to facilitate the firing process. Sometimes when soles have been added, and the arms do not have holes at the arm-pit, as was usual, holes have been drilled into each arm and leg to let the gases escape.

Buckled Shoes

There is no truth in the rumour that the eighteenth century Tobies tend to have buckles on their shoes rather than laces. Although buckles went out of fashion in the early nineteenth century, it must be remembered that in the main they were used primarily by the gentry, and the ordinary man would have laced his shoes.

The Smoking Pipe

The presence of a pipe is usually a good sign, but it must be part of the original jug and not a later addition. Some ordinary Victorian Tobies have a crudely modelled pipe lying along the right arm which is supporting the jug on the knee. Pipes were often an added feature, most commonly held in the right hand (which is supporting the bottom of the jug) or down by Toby's right leg, (not usually the left leg). Rarer still is a pipe situated between the legs or in the mouth, and this can often be used as an indication that the Toby is an early one. Beware that the pipe has not been added at a later date!

Smoking Pipe Toby, c1790

The Base

Eighteeth century bases vary in thickness from ⅜" to 1⅝" — often with concaved corners.

This base is the most common throughout all periods.
Recess: approx ¼"

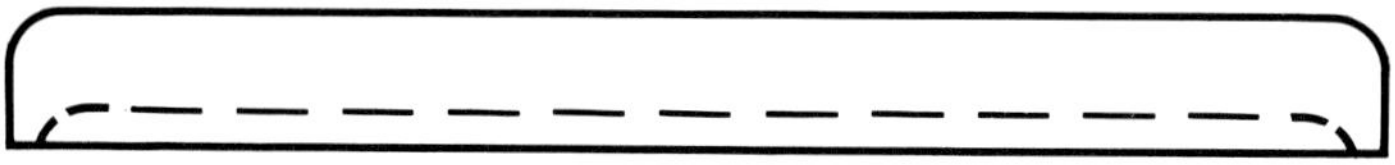

Eighteenth Century Base: Recess approx ⅝"-1" deep

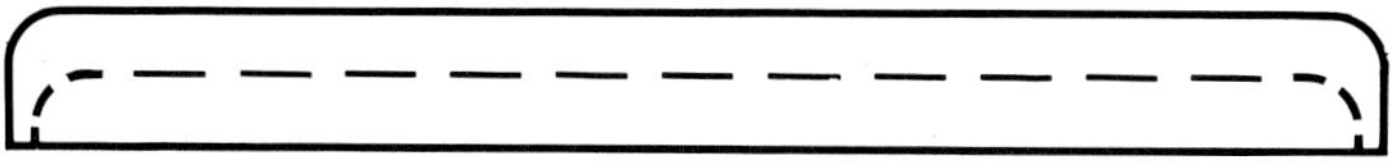

Eighteenth Century Base: Flat Bottom — no Recess

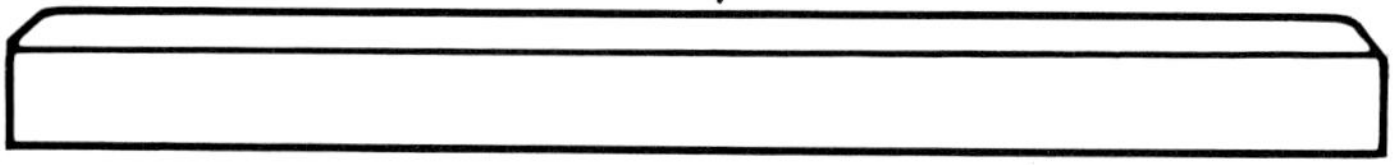

Eighteenth Century up to c1840 'Step Toby'

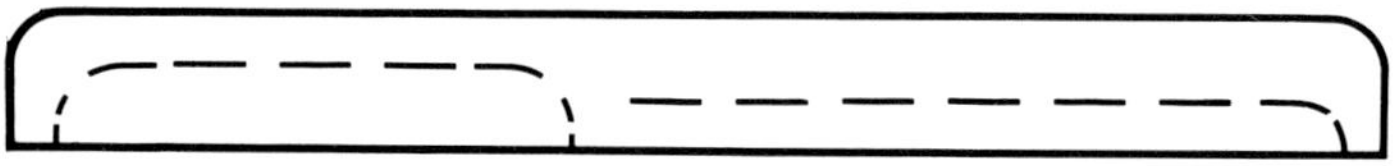

The 'step' Toby is so called because the recess is deeper at one end than the other.

Some Georgian Tobies have a raised floral decoration around the base thus:

The underside of the base of the eighteenth century coloured glaze Tobies are often completely unglazed or only glazed in part. It was probably thought unnecessary to glaze the bottom, but the glazing may have been omitted in order to prevent the pot sticking to the 'sagger base' during firing.

A painted line around the edge of the base appears on late eighteenth century enamelled Tobies such as those by Neale & Co c1778-80 (contrary to popular belief that this was a nineteenth century innovation), but it is unlikely to be found on Wood jugs, nor on any of the Tobies with a translucent glaze.

A good way of testing the authenticity of what looks to be an old jug is to look through the top of the jug where the sides meet the base and check on any accumulation of grime and dirt. If the jug is old it will have accumulated over the years, even if it has been washed regularly (though few ever get a bath). Fakers do not usually think of this, not till now at least, so look for it when you are being sold 'the genuine article'.

Maker's Names

Before c1840 impressed marks were neatly set into the soft clay during manufacture. The exception is salt-glaze stoneware such as Doulton's which was produced after this date with impressed marks.

It must be noted though that 95 per cent of all early Tobies do not have any marks on them! Those that do bear marks are listed on page 106. But remember that although the mark is likely to be missing, the collector can develop his enthusiasm for Tobies by weighing up other indications as to the nature of the jug, by looking at the modelling, the 'feel', the glaze and other aspects aforementioned. However an early Toby bearing the maker's mark is a most desirable acquisition, it not only proves both the maker and approximate date of the piece, but it also allows us to use it as a guide to other unmarked jugs which have been made by the same potter. The presence of a mark thus adds value to the piece.

The most commonly marked pre-Victorian jugs are those marked 'Davenport'. These jugs were made at Longport, Burslem and the mark is usually impressed on the bottom of the jug with an anchor device beneath, though not all Davenport jugs are marked. On such jugs there are often two numerals showing the year of manufacture, situated on either side of the anchor.

The Davenport jugs are brightly coloured enamel Tobies, sometimes with gilding, and the bases are often stipple painted around the outside. This is also a feature of Portobello ware jugs and it is difficult to tell the difference between them since both potteries used the same kind of enamelling and colours and produced the jugs at around the same time c1830-40. Portbello jugs are unmarked.

See Chapter 7 List of Makers Marks.

Early Toby with barrel between legs c1795

An early 'Ordinary' Toby

Left, The Bargeman. Right, 'Ordinary Toby'.

Chapter Five
The Toby Family

The Toby is obviously more than a simple representation of Toby Fillpot (or Phillpot) the traditional British character. He has come to represent a piece of British culture, and for this reason the Toby now represents many different characters, mainly by occupation. They are indeed a 'family' of characters and their depiction in terms of Toby Jugs has ensured that they will not be forgotten for their contribution to the development of the British way of life.

The characters of the Toby family are many and varied and one often wonders just how some of their names have been acquired. Only three of 'The Family' of eighteenth century and nineteenth century Tobies have their names imprinted on the base; 'The Hearty Good Fellow', 'Lord Howe' and 'Nelson'.

The 'Snuff-taker', 'The Barrister' and 'Falstaff' among others, were given their names because they looked the part, indeed it may be considered to be an insult to the modeller if they had not been recognised as such.

Other names are derived from the various objects which may be held in the hands, like a bottle, a book or a bell for instance.

Others were given their names by early collectors, and rightly or wrongly, their names have stuck. Examples are 'The Nightwatchman', 'Prince Hal', 'The Tipsy Man' and 'The Squire'.

It must be noted that the makers mentioned in the listings are those currently known, and there may be many other potters of particular types.

The Bargeman

This particular character is very rare, depicting a seated man with an anchor between his legs. He holds a flask in his left hand and a glass in his right and is dressed in the uniform of a waterman of the King's barge. He has a short jacket and baggy pantaloons, and on the sides of the rectangular mound on which the bargeman is sitting are cameos of the head of King George III surrounded by festoons.

This is a late eighteenth century jug, probably in coloured glazes. According to records only three exist: one was in the possession of Captain Price, which was produced with a mottled mauve coat and which he thought had been made by Whieldon, one was on show in the Ideal Homes Exhibition of 1976 (in the Pavilion, commemorating the bicentenary of the American War of Independence) and a third Bargeman sold at Christies Auction Rooms in 1977, coloured cream, green and manganese. It is primitively modelled with gruesome teeth, the Toby is 9¼″ high.

THE BARGEMAN

Maker/s	*Date*	*Recorded Sales/Market Values*	
Unknown	18th C	Christies 1977	£500

The Barrister

This was first produced by Minton of Stoke-on-Trent in 1873. It is 11¾″ high, made in coloured majolica ware sometimes in polychrome colours also in Whieldon type running enamel mottled colours or plain white porcelain. It shows a standing man with his hands in his trouser pockets. He wears a typical barrister's wig with a tricorn hat on top and a long gown with a cravat around his neck. The jug's handle appears as a long pig-tail reaching down to his waist, bound with ribbon and tied top and bottom with a bow. Hanging from his right waistcoat pocket is a watch fob seal.

The Barrister in coloured majolica (left). Right, in white porcelain

A companion to this is a female Toby which is similar in size and colouring, whose hair combines to form the handle of the jug. She is dressed in conventional Georgian clothes and has her left arm across her breast, holding a fan. See under female Tobies, 'Lady with a fan'.

THE BARRISTER

Maker/s	*Date*	*Height*	*Recorded Sales/Market Values*	
Minton	1873	11¾″	Christies 1984	£900
			Beanes 1984	£1000

There is a copy of this Toby in the Minton Museum. It is dated 1891-1912, described as '18th century Staffordshire salt glaze' and marked with the black printed globe of Mintons, England.

The Black Man Toby

This is a Toby Jug which was potted around 1850 and was made at about the same time as the Staffordshire figures such as the 'Uncle Tom and Little Abner' which are associated with the American Civil War. They were produced as a political gesture against the concept of slavery.

There are three different types of 'Black man' Tobies. One is a standing man holding a jug in his left hand (moulded with the main part of the body). It is 9½″ high and made in bright enamel colours. Copies may be found with a cobalt blue hat (which is unusual for a Toby), a yellow coat and striped hose. It has a stipple sponged base and handle (probably Portobello ware). Only two moulds are used in production for the front and back of the Toby. There are also models of this jug in which the figure takes on the appearance of a white man, and there are modern reproduction of this latter figure. (See under 'Standing Man'.)

The second type of 'Black man' Toby is of the 'Ordinary' type. This was made a little earlier, c1840.

A third type of 'Black man' is a jug in brown pottery which has been painted in a blue/green enamel underglaze. The figure sits in the ordinary fashion with the jug on his knee and he wears an unusually large tricorn hat. The lips are negroid so one can justifably assume it to be a black man. It was made by C. H. Brannam Ltd. at Barnstaple, Devon c1900. It is usually marked 'Brannam Barnstaple' or 'Barum'. The jugs are quite common.

THE BLACK MAN (Standing)

Maker/s	*Date*	*Recorded Sales/Market Values*
Portobello (?)	c1850	More than £100

Standing Black Man in Portobello ware.

The Black Man 'Ordinary'. Courtesy of V & S Wright

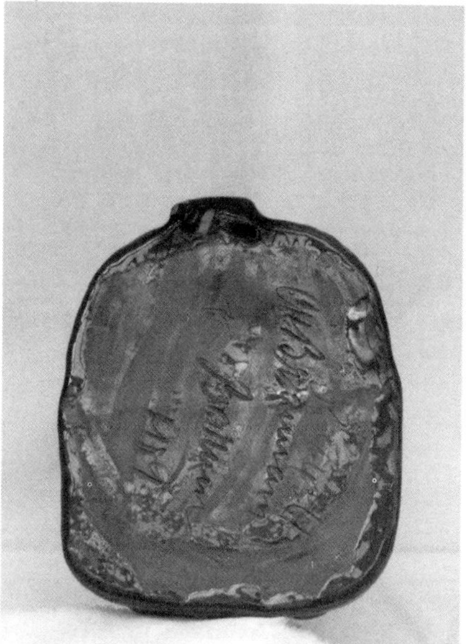

Black Man Toby potted by Brannam. Courtesy of V & S Wright

THE BLACK MAN (Ordinary)

Maker/s	*Date*	*Recorded Sales/Market Values*
	c1840	More than £100
C. H. Brannam	c1900	About £50

Bottle Toby

This is an unusual and very rare Toby which sold at Sotheby's, London, in July 1985. The seated toper has a lop-sided stare and is wearing a slate-blue coat, brown waistcoat and ochre breeches. Between his legs he is holding a 5″ high square shaped bottle. The jug had a rim chip and thumb restored and a replacement hat crown but still sold for £2,100.

BOTTLE TOBY

Maker/s	*Date*	*Recorded Sales/Market Values*
Yorkshire	18C	Sotheby's 1985 £2100

Far left and right, two Thin Man Tobies, the left with pipe, the right with glass. Centre, Bottle Toby. (Courtesy of Sothebys)

Bottle and Goblet Toby

In place of the usual Toby, with the pot in the left hand balanced on the left knee, a goblet 2¼″ high is held in the left hand and a bottle in the right. These Tobies are 10″ high in underglaze bright enamel colours. It is likely to have a half inch high recessed base and has the same characteristics of the Yorkshire Toby; the same facial details, the head inclined slightly to the left, the waistcoat opening at the top, and the ten buttons down the length of the coat. The handle of the jug is also in the same large proportions as the Yorkshire Toby, but is is not in a human form.

It is evident that these jugs were made in Yorkshire around 1800. This Toby can be found with the bottle resting either on the right knee or the left, though still held in the right hand.

There is also said to be a Toby of this form in brown salt glaze stoneware.

BOTTLE AND GOBLET

Maker/s	*Date*	*Recorded Sales/Market Values*	
Yorkshire	18C	Sotheby's 1980	£320

Bottle and Pipe Toby (Courtesy of Terry Ledwith)

Bottle and Goblet Toby

Bottle and Pipe Toby

This is very similar to the above mentioned Toby and was probably made by the same pottery in Yorkshire c1800. The goblet has been replaced by a 3¼″ pipe, the bowl of it resting on the left knee.

BOTTLE AND PIPE TOBY

Maker/s	*Date*	*Recorded Sales/Market Values*
Yorkshire	18C	more than £300

The Cakes and Ale Toby

Cakes and Ale Toby

It is thought that this Toby was modelled on Shakespeare's 'Twelfth Night' character, Sir Toby Belch, who had a fondness for cakes and ale. One Whieldon type miniature depicts Toby holding a glass in the right hand and a dish of cakes in the left. The Toby wears a green coat, yellow breeches and a tortoiseshell tricorn hat and is very rare.

Another model shows a seated gallant in a brown tricorn hat, yellow jacket and grey breeches, holding cakes and ale with a brown dog begging between his knees. The handle forms a knarled green bough on a square rock work base, 10½″ high, c1785.

CAKES AND ALE

Maker/s	*Date*	*Recorded Sales/Market Values*
unknown	18C	more than £300

The Cavalier

The Cavalier was a dashing, swashbuckling supporter of King Charles I in the English Civil War of 1642-51.

The Cavalier sits in a chair with his left hand resting on his sword hilt and his right on the arm of the chair. This is one of the few Tobies in which the figure sports a beard and moustache. He wears a large brimmed hat which is swept up on the right-hand side in order to accommodate a feather. It is a poorly modelled jug made c1900 in overglaze colours and is quite common.

THE CAVALIER

Maker/s	*Date*	*Recorded Sales/Market Values*
William Kent	c1900	More than £50

The Collier

The Collier is the traditional British coal miner having a drink after his stint in the pit. He was renowned for his drinking habits which developed as a result of his dusty existence.

It is difficult to be precise about the prerequisites for 'The Collier'. Lord Mackintosh, a famed collector, suggested that he could be an 'Ordinary' type Toby with a black or near black coat, but early Tobies

The Cavalier

The Collier c1780

with black coats are rare, and 'The Collier' may have any colour of coat. 'The Collier' should be so called because his face and hands are of a dark or dirty complexion. This dirtiness is often confused in auction rooms, the Tobies being catalogued as 'probably meant to be Negro'. The height is 10″ and the base often has a raised floral pattern around it, the corners being concave.

These Tobies can be found with a small barrel standing between the Collier's feet, or he might be smoking a pipe held in his right hand. These jugs have been made both in coloured glazes and in enamel colours under a clear glaze. They were probably not made after 1800.

THE COLLIER

Maker/s	*Date*	*Recorded Sales/Market Values*	
Unknown	18C	1984	£750
Yorks type		1984	£750

The Convict. c1780
Courtesy of Sothebys

The Convict

This is an 'Ordinary' type of Toby wearing a brightly striped coat with broad arrows painted on it. These jugs are rare and Captain Price illustrated one in his book, (see under 'Further Reading'), though no 'broad arrows' can be discerned on his coat. However, the one illustrated here has a broad arrow decoration.

THE CONVICT

Maker/s	*Date*	*Recorded Sales/Market Values*
Unknown	c1800	None applicable

Four Cornered Hat Toby, Davenport c1840.
(Courtesy of V & S Wright)

Cross Legged Toby. Gold Lustre c1850.
(Courtesy of V & S Wright)

Cross Legs 10½". Probably by Davenport c1840.

Cross Leg Toby. Probably by Sampson Smith
1850

The Cross Legged Toby

There are four different types of these Tobies. All of them hold a jug to the chest in both hands, like a squirrel holding a nut. The most common is probably the jug which was first made by Sampson Smith of Longton (Potting 1846-1878), mould no 3584.

These jugs have a vacant look about the face with lips and teeth painted in red. The stockings are usually painted with a vertical chain pattern and stripes, and the jug which he holds has a floral pattern around it.

This Toby was also made by William Kent of Burslem in the last quarter of the nineteenth century and was still in the catalogue (No. 370) as late as 1962, listed as, 'The Jolly Miller'. The jug is 8″–9″ high, the figure standing on a rocky mound, usually with a coat which is underglaze cobalt blue, overglaze red, or black. The hats are either red or black with a red or yellow band around the brim. They are often found with the hat crown still intact with a trilby type cleft. These Tobies are very common, but are more unusual if they have a blue willow pattern coat.

Gold lustre Tobies of this model were made with no other decoration on them.

A very similar jug has been produced in two sizes, 8½″ and 10½″, but the head is turned slightly to the left and the hat is askew. The maker is unknown, but these are much more finely modelled jugs. The Toby shown here has a cobalt blue underglaze coat, yellow breeches, white stockings (with a vertical blue stripe and dots on them), black shoes with gilt buckles, a pink waistcoat, grey spotted neck scarf, a black tricorn hat with removable crown and yellow band round the brim. Again, Toby sits on a rocky mound with a red rustic handle at the back.

A copy of the smaller version of this can be found in the Brighton museum Willet collection. They date this c1820 and call it 'John Bull'. However, the bright gilding on the shoe buckles and the general style of the figure indicates that it was more likely to have been made at the end of the nineteenth century. Furthermore, John Bull was usually depicted with a curled brimmed shallow top hat whereas this Toby has a tricorn.

Davenport made a similar jug to this in which the hat has four corners to it instead of the usual three (the fourth being situated in the middle of the back of the brim). This Toby, a copy of which can be seen at the Stoke-on-Trent museum, has a blue coat, yellow breeches, a lattice pattern on the stockings and black shoes. In fact, this jug which bears the Davenport mark is so like the 'John Bull' type mentioned above that Davenport might well have been the maker of that jug too!

The fourth type of cross legged Toby is about 8″ high and is much the same as the others in design, but tends to be rather moon-faced with the mouth, eyelids and arched eyebrows painted in rather than modelled and he has what seems to be straight lank hair down to his coat collar. The jug is shown in *The Connoisseur* magazine of March 1904, and was called 'Simple Simon', probably made c1890. It is sometimes referred to as 'Silly Billy' in relation to the street droll, Billy Barlow, well known in the East End of London in the early nineteenth century.

THE CROSS LEGGED TOBY

Maker/s	*Date*	*Recorded Sales/Market Values*
Sampson Smith	1847-63	more than £40
William Kent	to 1962	more than £40
Davenport 4-cornered hat	c1840	more than £150
Head turned slightly to left	c1840	more than£150

The Drunken Parson (The Sinner or Doctor Johnson)

The creation of this jug is attributed to Enoch Wood (cousin of Ralph Wood II), though there is no evidence to support this view. It depicts a man sitting with a wine glass in his left hand and a jug in his right hand from which he intends to pour wine. He fails to achieve this, due to his drunkenness, and he looks to the right in a stupor with a leering expression on his face. His tricorn hat is askew on his head.

It is interesting to note that the parson holds the glass at the foot, between the third and fourth fingers, giving the impression that he has five fingers as well as a thumb! He wears a black coat and white clerical cravat but when the coat is of any other colour this jug is known as 'The Unfrocked Parson'.

It may well be that the inspiration for the Drunken Parson was a print by William Hogarth in 'A Harlot's Progress' (scene 6) in which a glassy eyed cleric spills his 'Nants Brandy' (of Nantes?) out of a similar funnel shaped glass.

The base on The Drunken Parson always has square sides and back, but has a rounded front, a feature which can be seen on 'The Night Watchman' which is also attributed to Enoch Wood.

THE DRUNKEN PARSON

Maker/s	*Date*	*Recorded Sales/Market Values*
E Wood	c1830	sold 1980 for £260
		sold 1985 for £410 (damaged)

The Drunken Parson c1830

Wood-type Earl Howe, c1795. Sold Phillips 1986 for £3,400

Another Wood-type Lord Howe c1795

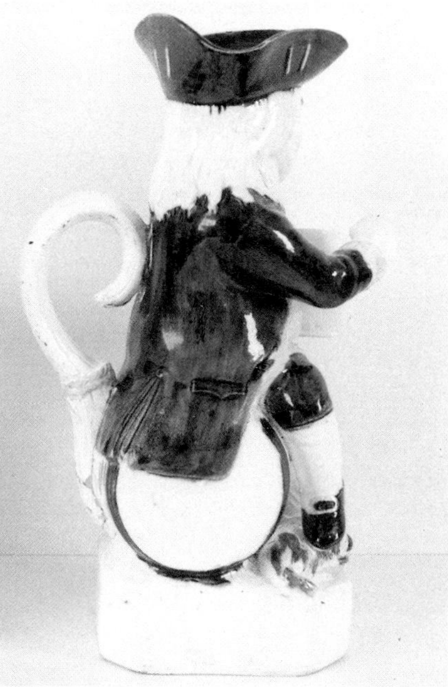

Two very fine Earl Howe Toby Jugs, Courtesy of D & R Ginns

Lord Howe

This is sometimes known as 'Admiral Lord Howe' but since 'LORD HOU' is inscribed on the base of one jug this is presumably the correct name. Richard Howe lived from 1726-99, and as Admiral of the Fleet 'destroyed' Cherbourg in 1758 and won a famous victory over the French at Brest in 1794.

At the end of the eighteenth century conditions in the Royal Navy became so bad that in 1797 squadrons stationed at Spithead (off Portsmouth) mutinied. The mens' demands were met after a one week strike, the dispute being settled by the one officer they trusted, Howe. He rowed from ship to ship carrying letters of pardon from George III and was affectionately known by his men as 'Black Dick'. Why such a colour should be attributed to him is not known but it may indicate something about the way he dressed.

The jug shows Lord Howe sitting on a barrel wearing a tricorn hat clutching a jug of foaming ale with both hands. Under his right leg which is slightly raised, is a King Charles Spaniel — though some models are known in which the dog is missing. Resting on the barrel by Lord Howe's left leg is a church warden pipe. The jug handle forms a bunch of rushes tied with a rope. The coat is usually green, but blue, brown, grey, violet, pink and speckled brown have all been recorded.

This is a beautiful and very rare jug possibly made by John Wood, who in 1786 billed Saml. Dunbibben for three Toby Jugs sitting on a barrel for six shillings and ninepence. This might explain why many early Earl Howe jugs do not carry the inscription 'Earl Hou', being an addition after 1788 when he was made an Earl. It was probably never reproduced in the nineteenth century, although some other potters made copies in the late eighteenth century. A jug with a painted four petal flower motif around the base is likely to be one of these.

The height of the jug varies from 9½" to 10', some with a Wood mould number, '63' impressed on the base.

LORD HOWE

Maker/s	*Date*	*Recorded Sales/Market Values*	
Wood type	18C	1974	£420
	18C	1980	£720
		1985	£1,700
		1986 Phillips	£3,400

Falstaff

This is a Shakespearian character who features in both 'Henry VIII' and 'The Merry Wives of Windsor'. He sits cross legged with a mug of ale in his right hand and his left arm sticks out, holding a club which forms the handle. This is another of those few jugs in which the figure has a moustache and beard. The jugs shown here are finely detailed and very crisply modelled, but certainly one of the finest of this kind to be found, standing 10″ high in pale blue stoneware is the jug made by Reed and Taylor of Ferrybridge, Yorkshire (1843-50). It was registered on the 30th December 1845 and bears the diamond shape registration mark of 1845. There are two holes at the top of the hat to rivet a pewter-hinged lid. These lids are often missing and were probably not even fitted to most jugs. One has been recorded with a silver lid, hallmarked 1848, and there are others, made in white stoneware with the pewter lid.

Jugs like this were made in brown salt glaze stoneware and more commonly in enamel polychrome colours later in the nineteenth century. In this century they were made in cream enamel.

All the jugs seem to have the Greek key-pattern motif around the base.

There is another very similar Falstaff to be found in Majolica ware, by Edward Steel of Cannon Street, Hanley bearing the registration mark for 14th November 1888, though not all jugs are marked. They are about 9″ high in which the figure sits with his left arm over the chair. In his right hand he holds a mug which he rests on his right knee and he sits cross legged wearing white breeches and hose, a green coat, a pale yellow shirt with blue facings and a blue tricorn hat - though these colours will vary.

There is something faintly reminiscent about the Prince Hal jug here in the way the left arm comes out to form the handle.

FALSTAFF

Maker/s	*Date*	*Recorded Sales/Market Values*
Reed & Taylor		£100
& Others	to 20C	£20-£100
Edward Steel		£170-£200

Falstaff in white stoneware with pewter hinged lid

Falstaff in pale blue stoneware marked date 1845 by Reed & Taylor

Falstaff in majolica ware by Edward Steel 1888

Falstaff in polychrome colours. Late 19th cent.

Midshipmite Fiddler c1775 and The Tailor, both by the same potter, often called 'Astbury-type', courtesy of Sothebys

Three early versions of the George Whitfield (Nightwatchman) jug.

The Farmer

This is a traditional British character, much diminished in number by the onset of the Agricultural and Industrial Revolutions in Britain at the turn of the eighteenth century. He is in the pose of an 'Ordinary' Toby sitting on a wheatsheaf holding a foaming jug of ale on his right knee (an unusual feature which is common to this character). He wears his hair with a fringe and his shoes have buckles on them.

The jug was made in Musselburgh near Edinburgh c1820-30, and can be seen in the Royal Scottish Museum.

THE FARMER

Maker/s	*Date*	*Recorded Sales/Market Values*
Musselburgh	c1820-30	more than £300

The Fiddler and Midshipmite Group (The Rodney Toby and The Farrier)

Some collectors consider these not to be Toby Jugs at all, mainly because they deviate so much from the standard 'Ordinary' type. The very primitive modelling which has gone into them indicates that they could be very early and the name of Astbury has been linked with these Tobies, which would certainly date them before his death in 1743. Such an association would put them among the first of the British Tobies to be made, but they could also have been made at a later date by an inferior potter. They care called 'Astbury' or 'Astbury-type', because they are thought to resemble his tiny figures which are primitively modelled with black staring eyes, but this resemblance is very slight indeed.

The Tobies in this group are mainly of men playing violins and viola de gambas. In the case of the 'Midshipmites' they hold sword drawn from a scabard and have a glass in the left hand. Variations of this group include an ironing Toby or "The Tailor" as he is popularly known and "The Farrier" (a blacksmith who shoes horses), wearing an apron and holding a pair of pincers. A Toby which has a glass in one hand and a jug in the other is most reminiscent of the 'Ordinary' Toby, but it is very easy to see that it could not have been inspired by the Dighton mezzotint.

The 'Rodney Jug' really dates this group of Tobies. Lord Rodney lived from 1718 to 1792, and in 1782 he defeated the French navy in a famous sea-battle in the West Indies. It is thought that all the commemoratives to him were made after this date, so if this Toby was made by the same potter as the rest of the Tobies in this group, they must all have been made at around 1782. The jug itself is unmarked, but mugs incised with 'Success to Lord Rodney' (and also some Loving Cups) have identical features, and it is this association which gives the Toby its name.

In spite of this, the rarity of these jugs, as well as their fetching naivety, makes them command a higher price than any other Toby Jug, whatever the quality. The Rodney Jugs are particularly rare, with only seven known to exist and at 11¾" they are more than twice the size of the others in this group.

Whilst there is no real justification for calling them 'Astbury-type', it seems that this description will stay until the potter is known — which is unlikely.

MIDSHIPMITE (Ironing — Tailor)

Maker/s	*Date*	*Recorded Sales/Market Values*
Unknown	c1780	More than £4000

MIDSHIPMITE (Fiddler)

Maker/s	*Date*	*Recorded Sales/Market Values*
Unknown	c1780	1980 Christies £3,000 Restored

THE FARRIER

Maker/s	*Date*	*Recorded Sales/Market Values*
Unknown	late 18C	more than £3000

RODNEY TOBY

Maker/s	*Date*	*Recorded Sales/Market Values*
Not Known	Late 18C	More than £5,000

George Whitfield Toby (Nightwatchman)

Whoever bestowed the name 'The Nightwatchman' on this jug got it all wrong. The clothes and wig are too refined to have been worn by a nightwatchman. It is far more likely to be the figure of George Whitfield, a famous Methodist preacher (1714-70) who was a friend of John Wesley. The reason for this possibly is that in Joseph Reed's play 'The Register Office', produced in 1761, Whitfield is introduced as 'Mr Watchlight'. The lantern was symbolic of his lifelong fight to proclaim 'The Light of the World', and in fact Whitfield was well known for his sermons which were often made at night, under the light of a lamp. This could have been the reason for his confusion with a nightwatchman. Another tell-tale sign which points to the fact that it is

Whitfield, is that he is known to have had a squint due to an attack of measles when a boy, and this squint is reproduced in his face (though not always apparent in later reproductions).

Of all the Toby Jugs made, this is surely the most unusual. Instead of the more conventional figure standing or sitting, with the tricorn hat acting as a spout, this figure sits on a chair holding a lantern in his right hand which is down between his feet, his left hand clutching a broad brimmed hat to his chest. His head carries a full bottomed wig known as a 'physical' c1780 — the same type as that worn by 'The Drunken Parson'. The back of the chair acts as the jug's spout and the handle is formed by the right hand holding the lantern. The figure is usually wearing a long coat which flows over the plinth which is usually marbled, splashed with a stippled pattern, or plain with a red-brown line around it. The figure is in both over and underglaze colours and stands 9½″ high.

A smaller version of this jug stands 8″ high. It differs in that the lantern is resting on the figure's left knee instead of the floor between his legs. There are two different models of the jug, the earliest and rarest being a figure with the smaller lantern, being held by both hands at the base. The slightly later jug has a larger lantern which is held by the Nightwatchman halfway up its side with the left hand, the right hand resting on top.

The white base has flat sides and back with a rounded front like 'The Drunken Parson' thought to be made by Enoch Wood. Enoch Wood also made very fine pottery busts of both George Whitfield and John Wesley.

The larger figure continued to be reproduced right through the nineteenth and twentieth centuries.

GEORGE WHITFIELD (NIGHTWATCHMAN)

Maker/s	*Date*	*Recorded Sales/Market Values*
Enoch Wood	c1800-18	
	30	£100

Mr Gladstone

This is a Toby of William Gladstone (1809-1898), who was British Prime Minister four times. Sitting with his back to a tree trunk which forms the main body of the jug, he holds an axe which is resting between his legs. This refers to his enthusiasm for chopping down a 'tree a day'. The jug was made by Sampson Smith at Longton c.1870. Although it is not a particularly impressive piece of pottery it is quite rare.

MR. GLADSTONE

Maker/s	*Date*	*Recorded Sales/Market Values*
Sampson Smith	c1870	More than £75

Hands in Pockets Toby

This is a standing man, quite similar to 'The Snuff Taker', but both of his hands are thrust into his waistcoat pockets. The figure wears a blue coat, red breeches, blue hose and a white waistcoat which is often lined with bright gilt and decorated with gilt dots and stars. He wears a black tricorn hat and has a silly grin on his face.

The jug stands 9¾″ high, is quite common, and some models have the letter 'R' impressed on the bottom. It is interesting to note that this is probably the only Toby, apart from 'The Barrister', in which the figure has both hands in his pockets.

Hands in Pockets Toby. Courtesy of Terry Ledwith

HANDS IN POCKETS

Maker/s	*Date*	*Recorded Sales/Market Values*
Unknown	c1900	£30-£50

The Hearty Good Fellow

This jug is also known as 'The Old English Gentleman' and is in the form of a man standing on a rustic mound with a tree trunk at his back, a branch of which forms the handle of the jug. The figure holds the traditional jug in his right hand and a church warden clay pipe in his left. He is dressed in a long cut-away coat and colourful waistcoat and it is the variations to the decoration of the waistcoat which makes this jug so interesting. He wears knee breeches and white hose and buckled shoes and the completion of this attire is the tricorn hat with detachable crown (although more often than not this is missing).

Other variations to look for in this Toby are:

1. **Trousers** in place of breeches and hose (these are early and very rare).
2. **The stem of the pipe** which may be running along the arm, or pointing upward across his chest, or it may be held in the left hand with the stem of the pipe in the mouth.
3. **A large jug of foaming ale** in the left hand instead of the pipe, balanced on the right fist, with the words 'Good Ale' written on the front. A similar jug of ale, with a glass in the left hand in place of the usual pipe can be seen in the British Museum. Marked on the back, on a scroll, is the word, 'Walton'.

Copies of 'The Hearty Good Fellow' were first made in the late eighteenth century, indicated by the coloured glazes, and they are very rare. They have been much reproduced, right through the nineteenth century and were still being made by William Kent of the 'Old Staffordshire Pottery' in 1962. The jugs without the inscription 'Hearty Good Fellow' are usually the earlier ones, made up to about 1840, though one may be seen at the Stoke-on-Trent museum, with the wording 'Hearty Good Fellow' on a white panel let into the front of the base. Impressed under the base of this are the words, 'Lakin and Poole' which would in fact date the jug as having been produced between 1791 and 1795.

In twentieth century reproductions the figure is squatter and fuller in the face than the earlier jugs.

Varying inscriptions have also been noted on the small jugs, such as 'Stingo', 'Good Ale', 'Success to our wooden walls' and 'Peace and Prosperity'.

The early known potters of 'The Hearty Good Fellow' are Lakin and Poole (1791-1805), John Walton (1818-35) and Neale and Co (1778-1814).

A Group of Hearty Good Fellows c1810-1830. NB. Inscriptions are omitted, indicating that the jugs are early.

HEARTY GOOD FELLOW

Maker/s	*Date*	*Recorded Sales/Market Values*
Lakin & Poole	1791-95	More than £500
Turner	c1770	up to £650
Yorkshire	c1800	Phillips 1986 £1250
Neale & Co	1778-1814	More than £600
John Walton	1818-35	More than £500
William Kent	c1890-1962	c.£50

Hearty Good Fellow probably by William Kent 1900 or later. Name appears.

Hearty Good Fellow in enamel colours. Sold Phillips 1986 £780. Courtesy of Justin Garrod.

John Bull

He is sometimes called 'The Landlord' or 'The Rent Collector' but the original John Bull (1523-1628) was an English musician who is believed to have written the earliest version of our national anthem. In the context of the Toby Jug, he is more of a bluff, good humoured, yet determined figure who personifies the characteristics of the English nation. This character was in fact created by John Arbuthnot in 1712.

He is depicted on transfer creamware jugs made during the last decade of the eighteenth century and also in the form of Pratt type jugs produced twenty years later. On these he is known as 'Boney and John Bull'.

The Landlord

John Bull by William Kent. Courtesy of Terry Ledwith.

The Tobies show John Bull as a sitting figure with a sheet of written paper in his left hand headed 'account' (sometimes omitted) and a bag of money in his right. He wears the knee length boots, blue coat and black shallow top hat which had been much popularised by *Punch* magazine in the nineteenth century.

William Kent of Burslem was possibly the sole maker of this jug in the nineteenth century, one being shown in his 1962 catalogue. It was first registered on 4th October by a Mr Gullic. This man's name appeared right through the year 1890, and it may be that he was a registration agent working for a number of potteries in production at the time. The registration number 153475 incised across the base indicates the year 1890.

This Toby is very common, but less so the variation with multi-coloured coats, such as those with a floral or star-studded decoration in subdued colours. The value of these is usually twice that of the normal coloured jugs.

JOHN BULL

Maker/s	*Date*	*Recorded Sales/Valuation*
William Kent	Late 19C	£80 with floral coat

The Landlord

This Toby is also known as 'The Publican' and was made c1850-60. It shows a man sitting astride a barrel which is marked on the front:

HOME
BREWED
ALE
1

The Landlord wears a blue underglazed coat more often than not but other items of clothing vary in colour and decoration and are in overglaze colours. Around his head is a garland of grapes and vine leaves and his grey hair is worn long, down to his shoulders. He holds a floral decorated jug in his left hand and a glass in the other. The base of the jug forms a grassy mound and at the back of him is a crabstock handle. The jug comes in three sizes, 9″, 11″ and 12″.

A variation of this is one Toby of a stern staring figure wearing a peaked hat. He has black eyebrows and moustache and sits astride a barrel, this time marked, 'Ale' at the front and 'Stingo' at the back. This jug is sometimes called 'The Postboy', is 9½″ high and was made c1890.

Doulton of Lambeth (better known since 1913 as Royal Doulton) made brown saltglaze Tobies of men on barrels between 1870 and 1880, one type bearing the mark 'XXX'.

THE LANDLORD

Maker/s	*Date*	*Recorded Sales/Valuation*
Unknown	1850-60	Approx £60
Doulton	1870-80	More than £100

Large Hands Toby

This is an 'Ordinary' Toby, sitting, who possesses unusually large and ungainly arms and hands. In his left hand he holds a glass which is balanced on his right knee which is unusual for an ordinary Toby. It is usually yellow with incised rings round the neck. This character has a smiling almost girlish face and a pigtail at the back of his head and wears a coat which is almost always a reddy brown. The head and hat are rather large and the jug usually has its large bulbous detachable hat crown intact. The handle is of the rustic type.

These jugs come in different sizes, from 7″ to 11″ high. They are glazed in bright enamel colours and are often thought to be rare, even unique, but this is something of a misnomer, because there are a number of these jugs around.

LARGE HANDS TOBY

Maker/s	*Date*	*Recorded Sales/Valuation*
Unknown	c1800	More than £400

Large Hands Toby

Roman Nose Toby. Courtesy of D & R Ginns.

Long Face Toby, Sharp Face Toby and Roman Nose Toby (the Wood variations)

'Long face' is the 'Ordinary' type Toby, but with a longer face. It is difficult to describe, so it's best to compare with a photograph along side an 'Ordinary'. Most long face Tobies are of the drinking type (glass raised in the right hand) and all of them are thought to be by Ralph Wood, though the evidence for this is somewhat circumspect. There is also the non-drinking 'Long Face Toby', one of which may be found with 'Ale' printed on the small jug, but this is most unlikely to be made by Ralph Wood.

The 'Sharp Face Toby' has a chubby face, but with the thin hooked nose of the drinking type, and is again unlikely to be made by Ralph Wood.

The Roman nose Toby is the Ralph Wood Shield Toby which has the same facial expression but no shield. All these types are rare and valuable.

LONG FACE TOBY AND SHARP FACE TOBY

Maker/s	*Date*	*Recorded Sales/Valuation*
Wood-type	c1790	More than £2000

ROMAN NOSE TOBY

Maker/s	*Date*	*Recorded Sales/Market Values*
Wood-type	c1790	1986 Sothebys £2400

Long Faced Toby. Courtesy D & R Ginns *Sharp Faced Toby. Courtesy of Sothebys*

Man on a Barrel

See 'The Landlord', 'The Publican', 'The Postboy' and 'Earl Howe', all of which are Tobies which sit on a barrel.

Napoleon

This was made in brown saltglaze stoneware by Doulton and Watts at Lambeth, c1825. It shows Napoleon standing, his left hand thrust into his waistcoat in characteristic pose whilst his right hand holds a small telescope.

NAPOLEON

Maker/s	*Date*	*Recorded Sales/Market Values*
Doulton	1825	£250

Nelson

Viscount Horatio Nelson (1758-1805) died at the Battle of Trafalgar aboard his flagship 'The Victory'. This Toby shows Nelson standing on a rocky mound with the word 'Nelson' printed on it and this mound rises up Nelson's back to form a handle. At his back is a black cannon barrel.

One version of this is an enamel jug painted in a very pleasant mottled brown with a yellow waistcoat and red breeches. Although the figure can be found with the uniform navy blue colours, it is more often than not painted with a yellow waistcoat and red breeches. There does not seem to be any justifiable reason for this, for we would expect naval men to be wearing navy blue.

There is a jug of Nelson in the Brighton museum, taken to be a mid-nineteenth century jug, but it is highly improbable that any of the jugs were made before 1866, the date of the completion of Nelson's column in Trafalgar Square, London. It was at this time that there was renewed interest in the sea hero. One is shown in William Kent's catalogue of 1910, and the Gladstone pottery of Longton was potting reproductions as late as 1975.

All of the above mentioned Nelson jugs are common.

Nelson, late 19th Cent.
Courtesy of V & S Wright

Doulton also made a 'Nelson' Toby Jug which featured Nelson in a tricorn hat and dressed in a bottle-green uniform. He wears a pig-tail which forms the handle of the jug.

NELSON

Maker/s	*Date*	*Valuation*
Doulton	1870	More than £200
Pratt	1870	More than £200
Kent	c1900	£50

Nightwatchman

See under George Whitfield Toby

One Armed Toby

The 'One Armed Toby' has never been designed as such, there being no record of Tobies actually modelled with one arm or hand. A number of early Tobies did however suffer the loss of an arm or a hand before the gloss firing process. This has thus given the impression that the 'One Armed Toby' was intentionally made this way with the glaze running over the broken limb. In spite of this the effect is not totally realistic because one would expect that the arm of the Toby's sleeve would be pinned back or rolled up. One might also expect there to be a hook or something where the stub of the arm comes out of the sleeve.

For a number of collectors these are still acceptable Tobies though, and they can sell for quite large amounts in auctions. Although in essence they are flawed pieces, the early jugs have good modelling in every other respect, thus maintaining the value of the Toby on the collector's market.

Pink Lustre Coat Toby

Some Tobies from around the early part of the nineteenth century were made in 'lustre' which became quite popular; copper, gold and silver lustre being fairly common, but pink lustre coats less so, making these Tobies something of a collector's item.

PINK LUSTRE COAT TOBY

Maker/s	*Date*	*Recorded Sales/Market Values*
Not Known	19C	Sothebys 1980 £800

Pink Lustre Toby, c1845.

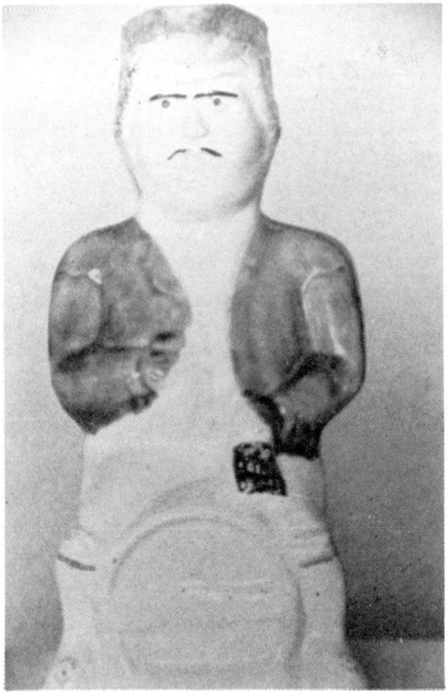

The Postboy Toby

The Postboy

This is a name given to a Toby depicting a man sitting astride a barrel. He has a stern, staring face and a black moustache with dots for eyebrows. He seems to be wearing a postman's hat of the style worn around the 1890s (when this jug was probably made). The arms and legs are an integral part of the body, so only two moulds were used to produce the jug apart from the handle. He holds a glass in his right hand and a bottle in his left. It is a poorly modelled jug but is quite rare. A picture of it appeared in *The Connoisseur* in March 1904, and it is reproduced above.

THE POSTBOY

Maker/s	*Date*	*Recorded Sales/Market Values*
Not Known	c1890s	More than £100

The Postillion

The Postillion was the common coach driver who used to ride the rear horse of a group of horses from the saddle, rather than from the top of the coach. This Toby is very like an 'Ordinary' Toby, except that the hat is a bicorn rather than a tricorn and he wears top boots rather than the usual stockings. He carries a jug of foaming ale in his left hand and a glass in his right (although one has been recorded in which the vessels were in the other hands), and the jugs were made in various colours, their height being around 7¼″. He has rather staring eyes with a distinctive pot belly protruding from his coat.

THE POSTILLION

Maker/s	*Date*	*Recorded Sales/Market Values*
Not Known	c1840	More than £300

The Postillion. Courtesy of W F Greenwood & Sons Ltd.

'Prince Hal Jug', early 19th Cent. Courtesy of Sothebys

The Prince Hal Jug

This is sometimes known as the 'King Hal' jug. It is a striking jug, said to represent Sir Toby Belch from Twelfth Night, or George IV who when Prince of Wales, masqueraded as Henry VIII at a Brighton ball.

A number of these Tobies were produced, one of the potters thought to be Ralph Wood. They are 14″, 15″ and 16″ high. The figure is always wearing a slashed doublet and a tricorn hat. In his right hand is a sword, his left arm forming the handle of the jug whilst his left hand holds a buckler, embossed with a crowned head and the initials 'G.R.', no doubt those of George IV. It was probably made to commemorate his coronation in 1820 and it is unlikely, in light of the high quality of the jugs, that they were made later than this date.

There are variations of this jug, one in which the right hand is holding a wide-topped, stemmed glass instead of the usual mug of beer and a sword at his left side with a tall jug resting on the floor. Another version depicts Prince Hal with his left hand holding his sword scabbard. The bases are usually square, sometimes with an acanthus leaf motif on them, and the figure sometimes stands on rocky ground.

PRINCE HAL

Maker/s	*Date*	*Recorded Sales/Market Values*
R Wood	18C	More than £2,500
Staffs?	c1820	More than £1,250

Punch and Judy

These are the only Toby Jugs which have been made to sell as a pair, and this breaks with the usual practice of producing Tobies as single items. Both jugs are around 10″ high and Punch usually wears striped clothes and a forward pointed conical hat (though this is often missing). He sits on a pile of books which are evidently volumes of *Punch* magazine.

Judy is also sitting, with her right hand in the pocket of her costume and her left hand holding a cane. She is sometimes dressed in a long white gown and apron, though she can also be found with a pale blue bodice and sleeves accompanying a red skirt. A third colour variation is an all yellow dress.

The Punch and Judy shown here have an impressed registration mark No. 139844 and the date 30th November, 1889. They were made by William Machin of Hanley, Staffordshire, the date showing when they were first made. William Machin went out of business in 1911 and it is possible that the original moulds were acquired by William Kent, a mile and a half up the road, in Burslem. They were then produced there and still catalogued in 1962 with numbers: Punch 381 and Judy 382.

There is a second Punch Toby Jug much less common than the above mentioned which was made in the middle of the nineteenth century, painted in bright enamel colours — black, blue, maroon, cream, yellow and green. It was possibly made at one of the Portobello factories, and stands about 8″ high.

PUNCH AND JUDY

Maker/s	*Date*	*Recorded Sales/Market Values*
W. Machin	c.1889-1910	£75
W. Kent	c.1910-1962	£50

Prince Hal 18th Century Wood-type

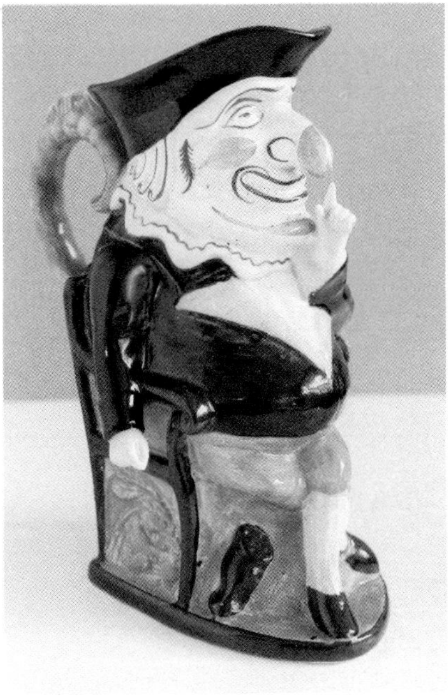

Punch, c1850. Portobello. Courtesy D & R Ginns

Punch by W Kent. Courtesy of Terry Ledwith.

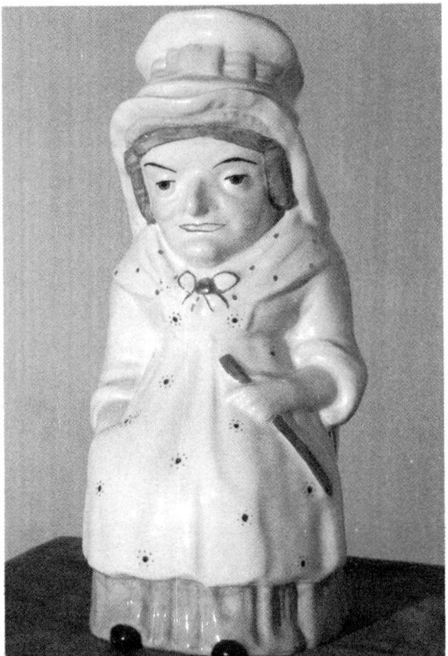

Judy by W Kent. Courtesy of Terry Ledwith.

Puzzle Jug Toby

This is a very rare Toby with spouts or tubes in three corners of Toby's tricorn hat. Working on the same principle as the traditional puzzle jug made in Medieval times, the drinker must block off two of the tubes and the hole at the inside of the handle, the liquid being sucked up through the third tube. If the wrong tube is sucked, the liquid flows out onto the imbiber through the side of the jug, which is pierced.

The jug was made in Yorkshire and impressed with a crown mark. Toby holds a jug on the left knee and the handle is of the figure head type.

PUZZLE JUG TOBY

Maker/s	*Date*	*Recorded Sales/Market Values*
Yorks	c.1790-1810	More than £750

Left Sailor c1790. Centre Puzzle Jug c1800. Right Hearty Good Fellow, Pratt-type wearing trousers. Courtesy of Christies.

The Reading Toby

First listed by Captain Price, this Toby is very rare indeed and of unknown origin. It is a Toby holding an open book in both hands, and is beautifully modelled, being 11″ high. It is so rare, only the one being known, that it must be very valuable.

READING TOBY

Maker/s	*Date*	*Recorded Sales/Market Values*
Not Known	18C	More than £2,500

The Small Sailor/American Sailor

This is sometimes called, 'The Small Sailor', or 'American Sailor'. The former because it is smaller than the Rodney Sailor, or the latter because 'Dollars' is often written on one or both sides of the sea chest he is sitting on. The sailor is not American though, because on the jug which he holds is written, 'Success to our Wooden Walls', which refers to the British tall-sided battleships with their four rows of guns. When the inscription is present it is surrounded by a heart shape or a floral pattern, though sometimes the jug is all white without any inscription.

The Small Sailor sits on a white sea chest and is dressed in blue, though sometimes his trousers are white, with blue stripes down them. His waist length jacket is fastened by two rows of white buttons and he wears white socks with black shoes and buckles. He also wears a black scarf and hat with a detachable crown (often missing). The sailor's hair is gathered at the back of the head into a tarred pig-tail or 'queue'. The large overflowing jug of ale marked 'Success to our wooden walls' is in his right hand, resting on his thigh, whilst his left hand rests on his left thigh, holding a clay pipe. The base depicts a green, grassy mound and running up the back, forming the handle, is the trunk of an oak-tree, the branches of which flow over the sea-chest and down the sides of it.

This jug is in overglaze enamels and is 10″ high, probably made in the first quarter of the nineteenth century. Captain Price

'Small Sailor'

is known to have had a copy with a 'W' impressed on the base, indicating to him that the maker was Walton (1818-1825). A copy is in the possession of the Victoria and Albert museum which was dug up on the Isle of Dogs in London's East End. A further variation, larger than the above jug at 12″ high is one in which a sailor sits astride the corner of a sea-chest. He seems to have a gum-boil in his mouth, it being slightly swollen on one side. It is not very attractive, but sold at Neales of Nottingham Auction Rooms in October 1978 for £130. Another sold in 1985 for £350.

SAILOR

Maker/s	*Date*	*Recorded Sales/Market Values*
Walton?	c1820	More than £400

The Sailor (also The Planter or Trafalgar Toby)

These are the various names given to a very fine and rare Toby Jug 11½″ high, of a sailor dressed in white trousers which are sometimes striped. The coat is blue, the waistcoat red, and he has a black neck scarf, black wide brimmed hat, and black shoes with buckles on them. The number of stripes on each leg may vary from three on some jugs to fourteen on others and on one sailor the trousers are checked. There is also a small floral motif in the squares of the base and on the waistcoat.

The colours can vary on these and a distinctive Toby wears a blue coat, white trousers with blue stripes, a yellow waistcoat decorated with small blue rings and a white neck scarf with blue spots. The jug held in the left hand is painted in white and yellow with a floral spray. This Toby was made much later than the one above, about 1890, and the colourful decoration on the clothes disguises his sailor profession somewhat.

'The Sailor' sits on a high backed chair, under which is a sea-chest with handles at each end. In the left hand and resting on one end of the chest is a large jug whilst in his right hand is a raised glass. The base of the jug is of a rocky mound, washed by lapping waves, and between his feet is a sea anchor.

The variations noted are: **Coats;** which are usually blue, sometimes with white lapels, or light brown with blue lapels. When the coat is olive green, pale manganese or slate blue, the lapel are usually yellow, **Straw Hats**, which are like those worn c1800 with wide-awake brims — some were made with round dish — type brims like bowler hats, or in the tricorn shape with sharp upturned brims and detachable hat crown.

Lord Mackintosh had one of these with a churchwarden clay pipe resting on the front of the sea-chest by the left leg. Ralph Wood is

Left The Squire. Centre Shield Toby. Right The Sailor. All late 18th Cent. Courtesy Christies.

The Sailor — left c1900 — right c1800. Note modelling definition on early jug.

thought to be the originator of this Toby, sometimes with the mould number, "65", on the base. Inscriptions noted on Ralph Wood Sailors are: 'W.B.C. Old Toby Grantham' and inscribed on the back in beautiful letters is:

"Hallo, Brother Briton
Whoever thou may be
Sit down on
That chest of hard dollars by me,
And drink a health,
To all sealors (sic) bold."

And on another Ralph Wood Sailor is:

"Dollars jolly Jack Tar
Just come from far
Drink round brave boys."

Other potters made this Toby, though probably not later than c1820, the exception being a model thought to be produced by William Kent of Burslem around 1900. The model shown here is one of these and has had cracks painted on the underside of the base and around the legs, probably in an attempt to fake the original. One sure way to tell the difference is to check whether the feet are hollow or not. If they are, the jug is very likely to be an early one.

The Planter

When the model of 'The Sailor' holds a plug of tobacco in his left hand as well as the jug, the Toby is then called 'the Planter', although the sea anchor might still be down between his feet. It is argued by some, however, that only when the anchor is omitted is it called 'The Planter'. All these jugs are rare, but 'The Planter' more so, and is therefore even more valuable.

Sailor/Planter

Maker/s	*Date*	*Recorded Sales/Market Values*
R. Wood	c1790	More than £1,500

The Trafalgar Toby

This is a sailor which wears a blue coat, white trousers and a white waistcoat with blue horizontal stripes. He also wears a black wide-brimmed sailor's hat. 'Trafalgar' is engraved on the handles of the sea-chest which is situated under the chair. On the back of the chest, between the chair legs is a medallion of Nelson's flagship, Victory (all in enamel colours). It is suggested that this jug was made at the Wood factory c1815 and there is only one known example. The jug held in the left hand is smaller than usual.

TRAFALGAR TOBY

Maker/s	*Date*	*Recorded Sales/Market Values*
John Wood(?)	c1815	More than £2000

The Shield Toby

This is an ordinary type of Toby, 9¾″ or 10″ high in coloured glazes which has a boat shaped shield on the left side which has inscribed on it, 'It is all out, then fill him agian' (sic). The misspelling of 'again' appears to be common to all these jugs and in the Midlands "again" was often pronounced "agian". The face of this Toby may vary a little in that the nose may be 'snubbed' (as on the 'Ordinary' Toby) or of the large Roman nose type. Sometimes Toby is smoking a pipe. Ralph Wood may have been the sole potter and Lord Mackintosh was under the impression that there were only six in existence.

SHIELD TOBY

Maker/s	*Date*	*Recorded Sales/Market Values*
R Wood	c1795	More than £2,000

Two Shield Tobies with and without pipe c1795.

The Snuff Taker

This is sometimes referred to as 'The Benjamin Franklin Toby', owing to its said likeness to the eighteenth century American statesman, philosopher and inventor, 1706-1790. He lived in England for eighteen years and he probably took snuff, as it was the fashion of the time.

The jug is in the form of a pot-bellied man taking a pinch of snuff from a box held in his left hand. It is the most common of all Toby Jug types and it can be found in Rockingham treacle glaze, brown saltglaze, overglaze enamel, plain white and silver lustre (the latter giving a pleasing effect when slightly worn off, exposing the brown glaze underneath leaving a ghostly, ethereal appearance). He is generally modelled quite poorly, although there are some attractive 4″ versions to be found. Some variations have a spout rising out from under his pot belly which transforms the 'Snuff-Taker' into a teapot in the most startling manner (not to be used when your maiden aunt comes to tea!).

There are rare and very interesting stoneware versions of the Snuff-taker. Two jugs are notable because of their similarities and their differences. One is about 7″ high, holding a square snuff-box upside down at arms length, the whole jug being coloured and slightly glazed. This figure is inscribed on the base, 'A.C. Pope 1829', which tells us that the Snuff-taker has been in production since at least that date. The other stoneware Snuff-taker holds the square snuff box in the more conventional manner and is slightly different in that it is much harsher and brighter than the other, almost a majolica. This jug was not signed, but was obviously made by the same potter.

There were a great many makers of this jug over the years and there are consequently a great number of different types. William Kent of Burslem was making the Snuff-taker from c1900 up to 1962 (mould no. 390), and Allerton and Son had another long production run from c1859-1942. The Allerton Snuff-takers usually have some lustre and gilt decoration on them, the figure wearing a blue coat.

Another maker was Sharpe Brothers and Co. who made a Snuff-taker and a companion female standing figure in a long dress. This is in majolica ware with a glaze running up the figure, varying from yellow to green. It is a poorly modelled jug, made c1880. (See Lady Toper.)

It is possible to find a 6″ high Staffordshire enamel overglaze Toby in a blue mottled coat which is the same pot-bellied standing figure as the Snuff-taker. In place of the snuff box in his left hand, he holds a large pot and in his right, a foaming jug of ale. (See under Standing Toby).

Silver Lustre Snuff Taker c1840

Left Portbello Snuff Taker c1840. Right Snuff Taker type but holding a jug in place of the snuff box. c1840.

Snuff Taker. Courtesy of V & S Wright.

Snuff Taker Teapot.

All of these Snuff-taking Tobies and their kindred drinkers have a base which is adorned with a bacchus motif of vine leaves and bunches of grapes.

The Snuff-taker is very common indeed, and because he came later than the 'Ordinary' (from around 1820), it is difficult to find any that were made in the quality of the early period and as a result it is rare to find any that are worth more than around £50.

SNUFF-TAKER

Maker/s	*Date*	*Recorded Sales/Market Values*
Many Potters	c1830	£30-£50
Rockingham		£30-£50
Sharpe Bros		£30-£50
Allerton		£30-£50
W Kent		£30-£50
A C Pope	c1829	More than £100

The Soldier

This is an 'Ordinary' Toby which gets its name because he is wearing a long red coat with yellow buttons (for brass), yellow breeches, a black tricorn hat and black shoes, which all fit in with the clothing of an

Two Soldier Tobies with a slight difference in decoration on their small jugs. c1830.

eighteenth century soldier. His white hose has a number of wavy blue stripes running down the leg.

These Tobies may look as though the faces have lost their crispness, possibly through the use of old worn moulds, but the glory of this Toby is the very fine 'sparrow beak' Pratt type jug of foaming ale held on the knee. This is a typical jug style of the 1830s.

THE SOLDIER

Maker/s	*Date*	*Recorded Sales/Market Values*
Not Known	1830	More than £100

Squat Toby

This is the name which is given to the group of Toby Jugs where Toby is sitting on the ground with his legs up to his chest and crossed in front. One version of this was probably made around 1840 and produced entirely in copper or silver lustre. The earliest ones have a pink interior with a pink lustre wavy line around the inside at the top.

However, it is more common to find the jugs in enamel colours. These jugs were produced throughout the nineteenth century, and William Kent of Burslem still had them catalogued as late as 1962 (though these later ones are poorly painted and lacking in detail). All these Tobies are between 4″ and 6″ high.

Some have a rustic type handle on them which may either have a normal handle top or one which is forked. The ones with the forked handle are usually the better quality jugs and are much more interesting.

There is also another Squat Toby in this group. It is a short, dumpy Toby made by Copeland Late Spode of Stoke. These are 6″ high and very colourful, in bright enamels with patterned/floral coats. The mark on the base is a sailing boat with a laten triangular sail indicating that it was made c.1900.

SQUAT TOBY

Maker/s	*Date*	*Recorded Sales/Market Values*
Many Makers		More than £50
Copeland	1894-1910	More than £50
W Kent		More than £20

The Squire

This is a most distinctive jug. It depicts a thin, gaunt gentleman with a beaky nose and long lank hair down to his shoulders. He is sitting on a corner chair wearing a long coat, knee breeches and hose, neck-scarf,

Squat Toby. Copeland late Spode c1900. Courtesy of Justin Garrod.

The Squire c1800. Maker unknow.

The Squire, William Kent c1900.

The Squire c1800. Maker unknown.

and buckled shoes. He clutches a jug of foaming ale to his belly with his right hand and in his left hand he holds a church warden clay pipe. The base is a very unusual shape, completely flat on the underside.

It is said Ralph Wood senior originally modelled this jug, and if one compares it to a portrait of his father in Frank Falkner's book 'The Wood Family of Burslem', one can see a striking resemblance between the two. However, with the speculation about Ralph Wood senior's potting status and his work for Wedgwood, we may now suggest that the jug was originally modelled by Ralph Wood II in the likeness of his grand-father — but perhaps this is going too far.

The hat crown and pipe are invariably missing from the earlier models. The early Squire holds the pipe in his left hand with index finger and thumb resting on top of the stem whilst the later nineteenth century Squire holds his pipe by the thumb alone. In twentieth century Squires there is no hole at all, even under the thumb, in which to place a pipe. Some potters in this late period have attempted to make a hole for the hand to accommodate a pipe but have not bothered to pierce the hole through properly, thereby dispensing with the whole idea of a pipe. This is an indication of the creeping decadence of Staffordshire pottery over time.

The Squire jug has been much reproduced in the past two hundreds year, one of the potters being William Kent (of the Staffordshire pottery) in 1910. These and later copies were made without the hat crown and without a pipe — not even the semblance of a hole between finger and thumb to hold it!

The eighteenth century Squire was made in translucent coloured glazes, whereas the nineteenth century versions had enamel cobalt blue coats or overglaze brown coats. These are the most common, but there are many variations. Sometimes underglaze mottled patterns are found which are quite attractive, and they are a must for the avid collector who cannot afford the original. These jugs were still in the Kent catalogue (no. 380) in 1962, and the Gladstone pottery of Longton was still potting them in 1975. A fine original of The Squire can be seen in the Victoria and Albert Museum, and another at the Stoke-on-Trent Museum.

THE SQUIRE

Maker/s	*Date*	*Recorded Sales/Market Values*
Wood-type	18C	More than £1000
William Kent	c1900	More than £100

Three Standing Tobies Left, The Black Man, Portobello, c1840-50; Centre, Modern Reproduction 1980; Right, White Man, Portbello c1840-50.

The Standing Man Toby

There are a number of types of this jug, four of which we concentrate on here. This jug is in the form of a man standing on a round stipple base, the whole in varying polychrome colours, about 10″ high.

There are recent reproduction models of this Toby which are quite good, but they are let down a little by poor painting on the face and heavy, exaggerated crackle. The reproduction model is a little smaller at 9″ high.

Another type of Standing Toby is 6¼″ high holding a jug in both hands. This little jug was probably made at Portobello c.1830 in underglaze enamels; blue, black, green and maroon.

A third, 6″ high, in Staffordshire enamel overglaze, has a mottled blue coat, which is the same pot-bellied standing figure as the Snuff-taker who holds the more traditional large jug in his right hand and a mug of foaming ale in his left. Another member of this group, again a pot-bellied standing figure of Snuff-taker origin is a Toby figure in enamel colours clutching a foaming jug of ale to his chest in both hands. He has a smiling face with a large upturned nose and stands 9¼″ high.

These Standing Tobies of the Snuff-taker type have a base in keeping with the ordinary Snuff-taker with bacchus motifs of vine leaves and bunches of grapes around them. See also: Black Man Toby, The Barrister, The Hearty Good Fellow, Nelson, The Snuff-taker and Rockingham.

STANDING MAN

Maker/s	*Date*	*Recorded Sales/Market Values*
Many Potters	19C	None applicable

The Thin Man

This is an aristocrat of the Tobies. As is implied by his name, he is a slender man, only 3″ wide and 9″ tall. He has a grinning cadaverous face and his hair has a curly fringe. He is wearing a tricorn hat, short coat, breeches, hose and buckled shoes and he is sitting on a Chinese Chippendale type chair. In his left hand is a brown jug, sometimes full, but more often than not empty and with his right hand he holds a pipe to his mouth. A variation of this is a figure with a glass instead of the pipe.

The jug is early, c1770, made in beautiful running coloured glazes. The copy shown here has a pale green coat, off white tricorn hat and

Thin Man with glass. c1780. Front and side view.

blue breeches and the modelling is superb! There is no degree of certainty as to who made the Thin Man; Ralph Wood, Whieldon and Leeds all having been suggested, but it is a desirable jug by any standards.

THIN MAN

Maker/s	*Date*	*Recorded Sales/Market Values*
Not Known	18C	More than £2,000

The Thin Boy

The name for this jug was first suggested by Eric Hudes in the 1950s and it is obviously made by the same potter that made the Thin Man. Instead of holding a glass or a pipe in the left hand the figure is steadying a jug on his knee. The face has fat boyish cheeks and the left hand side of the mouth is turned up into a leer. This is a very rare Toby indeed, even rarer than the Thin Man.

THIN BOY

Maker/s	*Date*	*Recorded Sales/Market Values*
Not Known	18C	More than £2,500

Two versions of the Thin Boy. Courtesy of Jonathan Horne (left) and Sothebys (right).

The Tipsy Man from the late Lord Mackintosh Collection. c1900.

Town Crier

The Tipsy Man

Lord Mackintosh considered that this jug was unique: the rarest in his collection. It is slightly larger than the 'Ordinary' Toby at just under 11″ high and the small jug is larger than usual, overflowing with ale. The coat is a beautiful soft blue-grey and on his head is a Top hat with a detachable crown which can be used as a cup. The chair which Toby sits on is unusual in that it, and consequently Toby's feet, are free-standing rather than on a plinth.

However, this is not a unique Toby, as Lord Mackintosh thought. A similar model is illustrated in Bernard Hughes's book, 'English and Scottish Earthenware', but it is not the same jug since it is a Portobello Toby, painted in polychrome colours beneath the glaze, and obviously made in the nineteenth century. By studying two photographs of the jugs it can be seen that they are remarkably similar in form, if not in glazing.

TIPSY MAN

Maker/s	*Date*	*Recorded Sales/Market Values*
Wood-type	18C	More than £1,000

Tithe Pig & Parson Jug

This is an extemely rare jug. It stands 10½" high and represents the Parson of the Tithe Pig Group, made by various potters including Lakin and Poole of Burslem in 1791. The original group shows a peasant farmer's wife offering her baby in payment of tithe instead of the pig held by her husband, whilst the Toby depicts the Parson standing, holding a glass in his left hand, almost at arms length. Inscribed on the yellow square pillar by his side are the words; 'I will have no child tho the pig'.

The figure has a detachable crown to the hat which can be used as a drinking cup.

This jug and 'Tithe Pig' figures in general were no doubt inspired by the following lines written in the eighteenth century;

In a country village lives a Vicar
Fond as all are of tythes and liquor
To mirth his ears are seldom shut
He'll crack a joke and laugh at smut.
But when his tythes he gathers in
True Parson then, no coin no grin
On fish on flesh on birds and beast
Alike lays hold the churlish priest
Hal's wife and sow as gossips tell
Both at a time in pieces fell
The parson comes the pig he claims
And the good wife with taunts inflames
But she quite arch bow'd low and smiled
Kept back the pig, held out the child.
The priest look'd gruff the wife looked big
"Zounds Sir" quoth she, "No child no pig."

There is a similar jug, equally rare, and now in Kansas City, Missouri, USA. This differs from the above mentioned jug in many ways, chief of which is that the Parson is not holding his arm outstretched and a large pig is standing by his right leg. In his arms he is cradling a pig. The jug is glaze stained with grey and splashes of orange and it is 10½" high, made c1770.

TITHE PIG & PARSON TOBY

Maker/s	*Date*	*Recorded Sales/Market Values*
Unknown	18C	More than £2000

Town Crier

This jug is in the form of a standing man holding a parchment in his left hand from which he is reading a proclamation. His right arm stretches up and out and he holds a gilt bell in his hand. The coat may

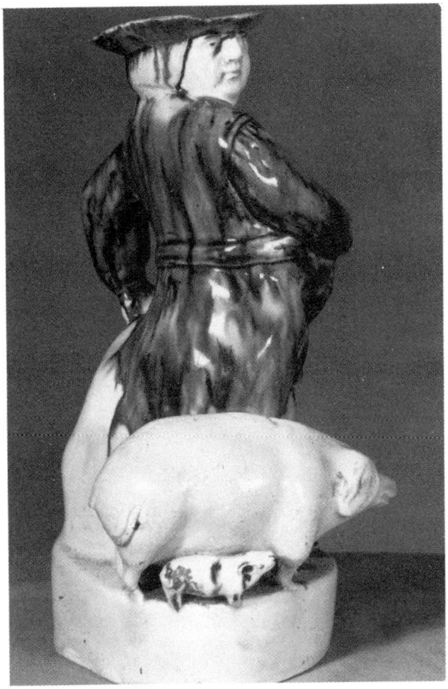

Tithe Pig and Parson Jug. Courtesy of The Nelson-Atkins Museum of Art, Missouri, USA. A gift from Mr & Mrs Frank P Burnap.

be brown or blue and the waistcoat is usually pink or yellow. The jug is stained in grey and orange.

These Tobies come in three sizes, 4″, 7½″ and 8¾″. Possibly made in the twentieth century this Toby is really outside the scope of this book since it is likely to have been manufactured in Germany or France, but there is a lot of confusion about it when it comes up for auction in Britain. These jugs are usually porcelain, Sampson of Paris often suggested as the maker and they are heavy, with a gold anchor mark under the handle. The Toby does not look incongruous in a collection of British Toby Jugs, and being unusual this makes it quite a collectors' find.

One other copy of this gives further scope for consideration because it is made of pottery, is 9½″ high and is quite lightweight compared to the porcelain ones. It has the gold anchor mark under the handle, indicating that it was made by the same potter as the above. The base has a 1⅝″ deep recess to accommodate a musical box movement.

TOWN CRIER

Maker	*Mark*	*Date*	*Recorded Sales/Market Values*
Sampson	Porcelain	Late 19C	1976 for £60
of Paris	Pottery	Late 19C	£100

Trafalgar Toby See under 'The Sailor'

Tumbler Toby

This is a brown salt-glazed stoneware jug of the ordinary type. Toby holds a tumbler in his right hand, similar in relative size to the pint glass we have today. His left hand rests on the left knee, the Toby being 8″ in height with the word 'Fulham' inscribed in free hand on the base.

A similar jug marked 'J. C. Fulham' is in the Victoria and Albert Museum, reflecting the name of James Carol who was working in Fulham c1885 so this may indeed be the same maker, though the style of the modelling of the above indicates that it might have been made much earlier, perhaps 40 years earlier. This does however indicate for us the maker of the quite rare stoneware artifacts that are sometimes found, marked 'Fulham'.

TUMBLER TOBY

Maker/s	*Date*	*Recorded Sales/Market Values*
James Carol of Fulham	c1885	More than £100

Tumbler Toby c1885

Showing Fulham mark on base.

Unfrocked Parson See under 'Drunken Parson'

The Village Idiot

This is basically an 'Ordinary' Toby made in the late eighteenth century with coloured glazes which are typical of those by Ralph Wood, though it is not thought to be by him.

The jug has been so called because of the particularly bewildered look on the toper's face. The potter is unknown.

THE VILLAGE IDIOT

Maker/s	*Date*	*Recorded Sales/Market Values*
Unknown	Late 18C	More than £500

The Welshman

This is another very rare Toby Jug, said to represent Sir Watkins Wynn, the head of a well known North Welsh Border family. He is depicted as a sitting man with a tricorn hat, his head turned slightly to the side. A goat, which is the Regimental mascot of the Welsh Guards, lies to his right underneath his striped-stocking clad legs.

The Welshman. Courtesy of Sothebys.

The Village Idiot. Courtesy of D & R Ginns.

The chair on which the Welshman sits has a sword and shield on the back and he holds a foaming jug of ale in his left hand balancing it on his knee in the conventional manner. The jug in hand is decorated with floral sprigs.

WELSHMAN

Maker/s	*Date*	*Recorded Sales/Market Values*
Not Known	18C	More than £1,000

Wineskin Toby

This is an 'Ordinary' type Toby, 11″ high, but instead of having the usual jug on the knee, Toby holds a wineskin over a brazier which is situated in between his knees. It is a great rarity, by an unknown potter, and it is not known when this was made.

WINESKIN TOBY

Maker/s	*Date*	*Recorded Sales/Market Values*
Not known		More than £2000

Two Yorkshire Tobies, the larger sold by Phillips of London in 1986 for £1,050. Courtesy of Justin Garrod.

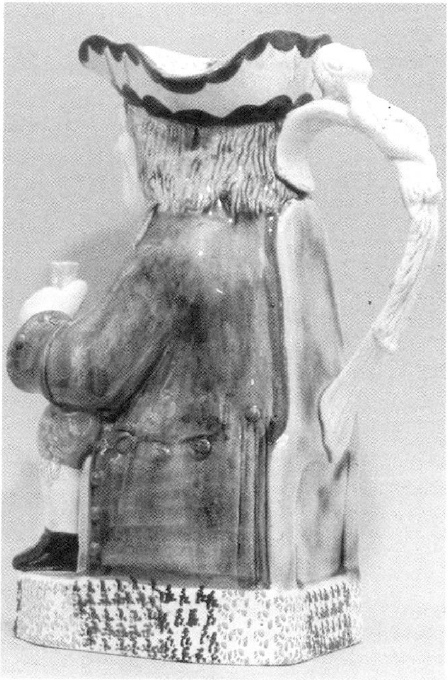

Yorkshire Toby showing handle. Maker unknown c1800.

Three Yorkshire Tobies c1800. Notice how the heads all slightly incline to the left.

Yorkshire Toby

This is a very brightly coloured Pratt-type Toby in enamel underglaze, about 10″ high. Many of these have a blue frock coat, yellow breeches and white tricorn hat, which is scalloped in black around the edges of the brim, though it is the sponging of underglaze colours on the base which is most typical of the 'Yorkshire' type. The hat is itself sometimes scalloped as well as the brim. The detail is more pronounced on some Yorkshire jugs than on others. Those that have the pronounced scalloped edged brim also have the unique feature of the Toby holding another small Toby, held in the left hand and resting on the left knee. He will also have a black and white spaniel dog between his feet.

A long serpentine clay pipe rests on either side of the Toby's chest, stretching from his shoulder to his pot belly. The back of the jug has a pale pastel green panel on which is fixed the white handle, which is a very handsome affair. The Yorkshire Toby handle is often in the form of a ship's figurehead, or a funeral type figure with arms crossed across the chest.

The eyebrows are usually a series of black dots, Toby sporting a tiny black fringe whether the hair on his head is black or brown. The hat and the whole of the inside of the brim has a stippled pattern in blue, green and yellow. This stippling is also on the detachable crown of the

Three very fine Yorkshire Tobies all c1800. Upper left showing serpentine pipe; upper right, with hat crown removed and below right, showing a dark red face. Courtesy of D & R Ginns.

hat and around the base of the jug. There are, however, many variations, as the illustrations show.

On many of the jugs there is a crown impression on the base.

In his right hand, Toby holds a raised six-sided glass. This Toby was made c1800. At one time, Sotheby and Co were referring to this jug as a 'Wilson Toby' because an impressed crown device like his was used by Isaac Wilson and Co 1852-87, but this was at least fifty years too late for these jugs. As yet no one seems to know which pottery used the impressed crown device and used the strippled pattern in blue, green and yellow. At one time they were referred to in auction catalogues as being made in the Don pottery but the Mexborough pottery, the Middlesborough and the Swillington Bridge pottery have also been suggested as makers.

It seems inconceivable that no one seems to know who produced the 'Yorkshire' wares as the output of this pottery was prolific in the production of Toby Jugs, cow creamers, watch stands, equestrian figures and others. Later imitations are common, with some of the same characteristics; the six-sided glass is in the right hand and a figurehead handle and a faintly moulded pipe on the body, but without the scalloped hat, small Toby Jug on knee or dog between feet.

YORKSHIRE

Maker/s	*Date*	*Recorded Sales/Market Values*	
Yorkshire	c1800	1986 Phillips	£1,250
Reproductions	c1840	More than £60	

A group of Toby miniatures, 4"-6" in height.

Left 'The Female Snufftaker'. Centre 'The Drunken Sall' (Davenport c1830). Right 'The Gin Woman'.

Chapter Six
The Female Tobies

The female Toby is not produced in anything like the numbers of her male counterpart, but where she is enshrined in the guise of a Toby she makes an interesting addition to any collection. In keeping with the tradition of the Toby she displays nothing of the beauty and finesse of the colourful fine china women so often produced over the last few centuries by potters attempting to immortalise the youthful women of their age. Not for us this age of sentimentality — the female Toper can drink as well as any man, and does. When placed side by side with him on the shelf we catch a realistic glimpse of middle-aged men and women drinking to happiness in one of the few real solaces of the time in which they lived.

Female Toby Jugs are rare in that only eight different female characters are known from the Georgian and Victorian eras, but of these characters, two were so mass produced that they are very common today — 'Judy' and 'The Lady Toper'.

Martha Gunn

Martha Gunn is in many ways the lady of them all, so it is worth spending a little time describing her. She is probably the only character whose notoriety is due entirely to the fact that her character and occupation was depicted in the form of a Toby Jug. Had it not been for her portrayal in this form it is doubtful that she would ever have been remembered.

In *The Brighton Journal*, 5th April 1780, the following advertisement appeared;

'To all bathers for the last thirty years, this is to acquaint the nobility, gentry and others resorting to Brightelmstone that Martha Gunn continues to bathe the ladies as usual, with James Johnson, a careful man with good horses, to conduct the machines in and out of the sea.'

Sea-bathing in the eighteenth century was not an easy business. The bathing machine was a small hut on cartwheels, and the services of a 'dipper' of the same sex was undertaken. It was Martha Gunn who bathed the ladies and she was described as, 'the venerable

Priestess of the Bath' by the *Morning Herald*. In 1806 the Herald paid the following tribute to her endeavours;

'The beach this morning was thronged with ladies, all anxious to make interest for a dip. The machines, of course, were in very great request, though none could be run into the ocean in consequence of the heavy swell, but remained stationary at the water's edge, from which Martha Gunn and her robust female assistants took their fair charges, closely enveloped in their partly coloured dresses, and gently held them to the breakers, which not quite so gently passed over them. The greatest novelty, however, that this part of the coast exhibited this morning, was a gentleman undressing himself on the beach, for the purpose of a ducking, in front of the town, attended by his lady, who *sans diffidence*, supplied him with napkins, and even assisted him in wiping the humid effects of his exercise from his brawny limbs, as he returned from the water to dress.'

In the same period Margaret Barton wrote:

There's plenty of dippers and jokers
And saltwater rigs for your fun
The King of them all is 'Old Smoaker'
And Queen of them, 'Old Martha Gunn'
The ladies walk out in the morn
To taste of the saltwater breeze
They ask if the water is warm
Says Martha, "Yes Ma'am if you please."

Five years later, amongst that nobility was the Prince of Wales, George III's son. For this reason there is a fleur de lis in the Martha Gunn hat and the doggerel;

To Brighton came he
Came George III's son
To be dipped in the sea
By famed Martha Gunn

The Prince of Wales first went to Brighton in 1785 when he was 23 years old and in that year Martha Gunn was 59. One cannot imagine why the rakish young Prince was being bathed by a 59 year old woman. Martha Gunn would usually bathe the ladies, but must have made an exception for the Prince.

The *Staffordshire Advertiser*, on May 6th 1815 printed her obituary;

"On Monday last, in the 89th year of her age, at Brighton, that well-known and esteemed character, as a bather, Martha Gunn of that town. She died on 2nd May, 1815 aged 88 years and is buried in St. Nicholas' Churchyard." Her grave can still be visited today.

Her headstone, which is surrounded by iron railings, reads;

TO THE
Memory of Stephen Gunn
Who died 4th of Sept. 1813
aged 79 years.
Also Martha Wife of
Stephen Gunn
Who was particularly distinguished as a
Bather of this town, nearly 70 years.
She died 2nd of May 1815.
Aged 88 years.
Also Friend, their son, who died 1st
of Nov 1784 aged 22 years.
Also Elizabeth B.L. their daughter
who also died 2nd of Oct. 1797 aged 30 years.
Also Martha their daughter
who died 27th July 1789 aged 30
Also Thomas B.L. their son
Who died 5th of May 1798 aged 37 years.

This then, is the story behind the character. She is depicted in the Toby Jug as a smiling female figure wearing a dress decorated with floral sprigs with smocking on the bodice, over which is an apron. On her head she wears a mob cap with a large brimmed hat on top (which is wider at the sides than at the front and back). The removable crown of the hat is like that of a bowler hat, but it is rare to find this still intact. Often omitted from the front of the brim is a relief of the Prince of Wales feathers, which are placed there in order to commemorate her bathing of the Royal personage in 1785. In her right hand she holds what appears to be a flask of gin and in her left hand a glass.

The jug was possibly made by Ralph Wood II in running glazes, and in enamel colours c1790. Other potters were producing Martha around 1800.

Oldfield and Co. of Brampton, Derbyshire also made Martha Gunn jugs in white stoneware c1833-1888, but these are not very impressive. Wood and Son of Burslem made a limited edition of 1,000 in 1973, 11" high and in bright enamel colours (see under 20thC Tobies).

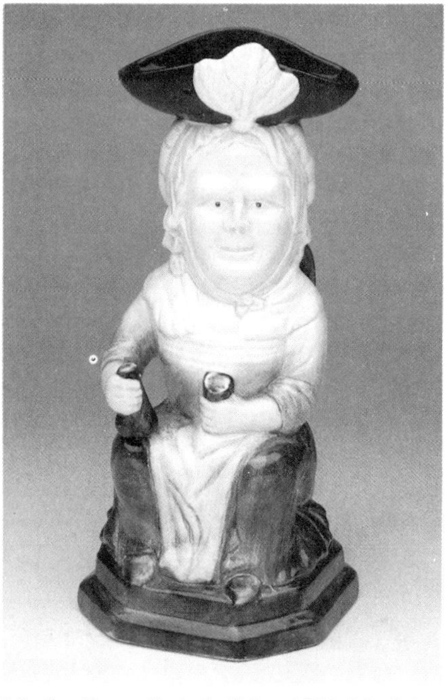

Martha Gunn, limited edition 1,000. Wood & Sons 1973.

Martha Gunn Pratt-type c1790.

Martha Gunn Enamel Colours. No.13 on base c1800.

Martha Gunn's grave Brighton.

MARTHA GUNN

Maker/s	*Date*	*Recorded Sales/Market Values*
R Wood	c1790	More than £1,000
Walton	c1810	More than £1,000
Pratt Type	c1800	Phillips 1986 £1,800
Oldfield & Co	c1850	More than £150

Drunken Sal

Drunken Sal is wearing eighteenth century dress and a large brimmed hat, typical of many Hogarth prints, representing the gin drinking woman of the time. The figure opposite shows Sal wearing a long white dress with a red, blue and green floral design which has been patched in ten places (as denoted by the black stitching on it). She wears a white mob cap on her head which is trimmed with black lace and on top of this is a large brimmed hat, the underside of which is yellow and trimmed with garlands of flowers. She has a torn blue shawl around her shoulders and her shoes are black. This is a very large jug probably only made by Davenport of Longport, Burslem and dated around 1830. The bases are often impressed with the Davenport mark, and the anchor and date numerals, but not always.

The jug depicts what can only be described as a sluttish leering woman sitting on a tree stump from which a branch rises upwards and forms the handle of the jug. From the base to the top of the hat brim the jug measures 12¼″ and the base is 8″ by 6¼″. She holds a glass in her left hand and a clay pipe in her right, with a semblance of smoke billowing out (the pipe being moulded in with the body and the smoke being represented on her dress).

In the book 'Nineteenth Century Porcelain and their Prices' published by, The Antique Collector's Club, 1982, there is a Drunken Sal wearing a black dress — which was very much underpriced at £40-£50! Two others appeared in *The Connoiseur* of March 1923. The jug is rare and very popular.

DRUNKEN SAL

Maker/s	*Date*	*Recorded Sales/Market Values*
Davenport	c1830	More than £350

Martha Gunn by Oldfield c1850.

The Hurdy Gurdy Player c1785.

Four Gin Women all c1840. Left Davenport, Second left, Copper Lustre, Third left, Rockingham ware. Right, pale blue, possibly Reed & Taylor.

The Gin Woman

This jug depicts a standing woman wearing the clothes which were fashionable around 1840, consisting of a crinoline skirt and an apron which reaches to half-way down the calf of her legs. This was the common mode of dress for the Cockney woman at the time.

Both arms are moulded separately from the body and she holds a glass in her right hand and a bottle (a flask of gin) in the left. These Tobies were made in overglaze polychrome enamel colours, 8¾″ high.

Another quite rare version is a very finely modelled Gin Woman in pale blue overglaze enamel, standing 9½″ high. They were more commonly made in Rockingham brown treacle glaze, about 8″ high. A fourth version is an 8″ high copper lustre model with a white glazed face, hands and bottle. It was probably made with all the others, c1840-1850.

GIN WOMAN

Maker/s	*Date*	*Recorded Sales/Market Values*
Portobello	c1840	Phillips 1985 for £100
Rockingham	c1840	Up to £50
All blue enamel	c1840	Up to £100

The Hurdy Gurdy Player

This must be the rarest of all the female Toby Jugs and like the Lady with the Fan, she has a degree of refinement about her that the others lack.

This is a Staffordshire jug c1785, 8¼″ high. It is modelled as a seated lady wearing a brown hat, yellow bodice and grey skirt, playing a Hurdy Gurdy. She has a monkey at her side playing a violin and the handle is in the form of a green dolphin on a rockwork base. It was found in poor condition, but was still worth £500 to a collector.

THE HURDY GURDY PLAYER

Maker/s	*Date*	*Recorded Sales/Market Values*
Staffordshrie	c1785	More than £500

The Female Snuff-Taker

Whilst the male snuff-taker is the commonest of all the Toby Jugs, his female counterpart is fairly rare. The jug was probably made at Portobello near Edinburgh c1845, and is decorated in typical hard bright enamel colours. A characteristic of this pottery is the use of maroon in the colouring and large green vine leaves on the base as decoration.

These jugs are thickly potted but with quite good facial modelling which has a bluish tinge welling in the creases, though the harshness of the colours, typical of so late a Toby jug, is not particularly attractive, and neither, judging from the expression on the woman's face, is the snuff she takes!

There is a further lady Snuff-taker (not illustrated) who is also standing wearing long skirts with her apron gathered up around her waist. She wears a type of mob cap tied underneath her chin, on top of which is a tricorn hat. This too is a little encountered Toby Jug c1870. There were many makers, but as with the male Snuff-taker they are post 1846 and are worth very little.

SNUFF-TAKER

Maker/s	*Date*	*Recorded Sales/Market Values*
Portobello type	c1850	More than £60

The Lady with the Fan

This is a female Toby standing 11¼" high, made by Minton of Stoke-on-Trent in 1873. The standing lady with her hand across her breast holds a fan and has long hair dangling down her back, forming the handle of the jug. It was made as a companion to the 'Barrister Toby', two of which were sold in auctions in the autumn of 1984 for £900 & £1,000. See 'Barrister' for colour variations.

Lady with the Fan
Minton. Late 19th Cent.
Courtesy Terry Ledwith.

The Lady Toper

This is a name given to another female Toby Jug. She has a pleasant smile on her face, no doubt in contemplation of the benefits of her lovingly clutched drink, held in both hands. This jug was probably first made in Derbyshire majolica ware, it having a glaze running down the figure in yellow and green. If it is a Derbyshire majolica ware jug, Sharpe Brothers & Co were probably the makers, in Swadlincote, c1880. The polychrome model was probably made by William Kent of Burslem at the end of the nineteenth century and was still in the catalogue as late as 1962.

The models of this jug tend to be quite poor, and are not really worth collecting unless one wants to build up a complete set of female Tobies.

LADY TOPER

Maker/s	*Date*		*Recorded Sales/Market Values*
Sharpe Brothers	c1880		£50
W Kent	c1900-62	10″	£50

Judy

The last in this group of eight known female Tobies is the wife of Punch. Punch and Judy were first made by William Machin of Hanley, Staffordshire on 30 November 1889. Across the underside of the copy shown is incised, in quarter inch numerals, 139844. W. Machin went out of business in 1911 and the original moulds were possibly acquired by William Kent, a mile and a half up the Waterloo Road in Burslem. Kent continued to produce them, catalogued as late as 1962 in numbers 381 (Punch) and 382 (Judy). Judy originally had a removable hat crown, which is more often than not missing, probably as a result of the ease with which it can be damaged. This jug is quite common and sells for c£50.

These worldly ladies certainly make a valuable contribution to the quality and interest of any collection, and though they may have interesting tales to tell, it is doubtful that they would be interested in coming home to tea to tell it!

Other Toby Types
(all one colour, miniatures etc)

All White Toby

An all-white or cream Toby jug may not sound very attractive, but when standing on a shelf of polychrome Tobies, these jugs look most impressive, especially if the jug is lightly potted with crisp, fine detail. The same can be said for brown stoneware, and they make a nice contrast when placed side by side.

Ralph Wood and Neal & Co. seem to have made all-white Toby Jugs along with other potters in the eighteenth century. As a result of their plainness these jugs never seem to reach the higher prices of their polychrome brothers, and can usually be purchased for around £100.

Brown Salt Glaze Stoneware Tobies

It would seem that no Toby Jugs were made in this ware before c1824, but once in production they were made in potteries all over Britain. Derbyshire was one area where they were produced, by potteries such as;

S & H Briddon of Brampton
J Oldfield & Co of Brampton, near Chesterfield
J Bourne and Son of Denby
Matthew Knowles & Son of Brampton
They were also potted by potteries in the London, Lambeth and Fulham districts.

The Toby type most encountered in this ware is an 'Ordinary' depicting a hooked nosed man holding a jug on his left knee with a fish-scale pattern on it. This Toby is usually 12″ tall, but also comes in sizes of 11½″ and 10¾″. They are not always marked but have been found with incised marks on them such as 'S & H Briddon', and 'M Knowles & Son'.

Snuff-takers are also common in this ware, see under 'The Snuff Taker'. A third, quite common figure shows Toby sitting on a barrel, which is lying on its side. This Toby is about 6″ high and can be seen in the Victoria and Albert Museum, but it does not have a handle, so it cannot really be classed as a Toby Jug.

The glory of most of these brown salt glaze jugs is that what they lack in colour they make up for in crisp modelling detail. Most of them sell for £70-£100, the possible exception being a large jug in which the Toby holds a fish-scale jug on his knee. These sell for around £200.

Brown Salt Glaze Stoneware Toby showing Fish Scale patterned jug c1840. Courtesy of Justin Garrard.

Brown Salt Glaze Snufftaker c1850.

Left, Earl Howe by Wood 1975. Centre, Barrister by Minton, late 19thC. Right, Ordinary Toby, late 18thC.

Rockingham Brown Treacle Glaze Tobies

The Brameld family managed the Rockingham pottery which was situated on the Earl of Fitzwilliam's Estate near Swinton, Yorkshire and they produced a manganese brown, lead-glaze Toby, and two examples of early Snuff-takers sometimes with the impressed 'Rockingham' mark on them. This type of pottery was made after 1826 when Rockingham first started producing this ware and although there are other producers, 'Rockingham' has become the generic term for this type of pottery.

These Tobies are particularly uninteresting in that they tend to lack detail, but the early ones do have a more attractive variation of colour tones. The later ones, made well into the twentieth century, are more uniform and dull. The Toby types in this ware are; the 'Standing Man' which appears to be the rarest, the 'Ordinary' Toby, 'The Gin Woman', 'The Snuff-taker teapot', and most commonly, 'The Snuff-taker'. The most one should pay for these jugs is around £50.

Miniatures and Tinies

These are Tobies which are not as big as the normal size, ranging from around 1½″ to around 7″, as opposed to the normal size of 8″ to 10″. Without doubt, the Ralph Wood miniatures are the most desirable to acquire. These are 6″ and 7″ versions of their larger brothers either with the right hand on the small jug or alternatively holding a raised glass. The bases often tend to be proportionately higher than on larger jugs, and of course there are many potters of miniatures.

It may help the reader if we look at some of the variations, but it must of course be realised that these variations do not account for all the miniatures that can be found.

The standing miniature, clutching a foaming jug with both hands to his left breast, is probably Portobello ware c1830. Where the standing Toby holds a glass and bottle which is moulded to his body, one has to use one's own judgement as to the desirability of the piece, since they have been made in great numbers from the 1830s to the present day. The bases on these are quite high and the Tobies vary in height from 2″ to 8″.

The small Snuff-takers range from 4¾″ to 5¼″ in height. One of the small Snuff-taker types is 6¼″, but he holds a large jug and a mug in place of the snuff-box.

Two very unusual miniatures of the Pratt-type Toby, made c1800, were sold at Sotheby's, London, in July 1985. One was seated on a rocky mound and was smoking a pipe, with a dog at his feet. The other was seated in a wicker-look chair, holding a jug and smoking a pipe. They were 4¼″ and 5″ high. Both were coloured in shades of

Left 19th Cent earthenware jug. Right, an early jug with 'running' treacle effect.

A group of late 19th Cent Snufftakers, all miniatures and tinies.

Left, Two ink wells, with pen holder in middle. Right, Mustard, Salt and Pepper (Vinegar is missing.)

Back Row, Left to Right; Jam Pot & Cover, Pratt Teapot. Pratt Pounce Pot. Spill or Pen Holder. Front Row; Egg Cup, Cup & Saucer, Reclining Fig Vase (Hat missing), Money Box with running glazes. Kneeling Toby Jug.

blue, ochre, brown and green, the former wearing yellow breeches. In spite of some restoration to both pieces they sold together for £1,200.

Tinies

The smallest of all the miniature tinies is 1½″ high. Most of these are of the standing Toby, but there is also a 'Judy', a man with his hands in his pockets, and a woman with her hands on her hips. The woman may also be found with hands over her ears or on her lap, or the man holding a glass up in his right hand. One might be lucky and find one of these little jugs with the Derby mark of the 'Stevenson & Hancock' period; made 1861 at the earliest. None of the above tinies seem to have been made before this date. Quite a number are made in porcelain and bear a gold anchor mark whilst others may be found marked 'Crown Staffordshire'.

It has been said that all of these tinies were made as traveller's samples but there can be no truth in this as they bear little resemblance to a full size Toby.

Chapter Seven
18th & 19th Century Toby Jugs with Known Makers Marks

C. Allerton	c1859-
Bourn & Son	c1809-
C. H. Branham	c1879-
S.A & V. Briddon	c1848-1860
Copeland and Garret	c1843-1847
Copeland (Late Spode)	c1894-1910 (sail boat mark)
Davenport	c1793-1887
Derby (Stevenson and Hancock)	1861-
Doulton (Lambeth)	c1870-
Fulham James Carol	c1885- (on brown saltglaze)
William Kent	1878-1962 (old Staffordshire ware)
Matthew Knowles and Son	c1835-1911
Hawley	1790-
Thomas Hollins	1791-1820*
Lakin and Poole	c1791-1795
Neale & Co	1778-1814
J. Oldfield & Co	c1838-1888
Reed & Taylor	c1843-1850
A. C. Pope	1829-
Rockingham	c1826-1842
Salt	c1820-1846
Thomas Sharpe	1821-1838
Spode	1783-1833
Swansea	c1783-1833
Turner	c1770-
Walton	c1818-1835
Ralph Wood (II)	1790-1795
Ralph Wood (III)	1795-1801

*Printed mirror-view on an 'Ordinary' Toby is TH 1794

Inscriptions on Eighteenth and Nineteenth Century Toby Jugs

'Ordinary Tobies'

'Mirson'	on base brown salt glaze jug
'O rare Dorset thou art my darling'	on base
'Tobey'	on base
'Charles Harding his Toby by God'	on base
'1793' a fake date on front of base	late 19th C
'John Barlow', on front of base	late 18th C
'Robt and Ann Wagstaff 1793'	around base
'Succefs to trade'	on small jug on knee
'Not for you Boney'	small jug on knee
'Honest old Stingo'	on small jug on knee
'Stingo'	on small jug on knee

Long Faced Toby

'Ale'	monogram on back of base

Yorkshire Toby

'William Manlay 1821'	on base

Martha Gunn

'Cheddar'	across base
'T. Burnell London'	across base

Nelson

'Nelson'	On front of base of Nelson

Shield Tobies

'It is all out then fill him agian (sic)'	on sheild

Hearty Good Fellow

'Hearty Good Fellow'	on front
and 'Stingo'	on small jug
'Good Ale'	on small jug
'Success to our wooden walls'	on small jug
'Peace and Prosperity'	on small jug

Landlord Toby

'Home brewed ale'	on front of barrel

A Toby sitting on a barrel on one end is inscribed 'Ale' and on the other, 'Stingo'; probably 'The publican'.

Sailor

Wood-type glazed Sailor:
'Dollars, jolly Jack Tar just come from far, drink round brave boys'.

On another Wood-type Sailor:
'Hallo, Brother Briton
Whoever thou may be
Sit down on that chest of
Hard dollars by me
And drink a health
To all sealors (sic) bold'.

On a third:
'Visct Jarvis', inscribed on the base.

On a fourth:
W.B.C. 'Old Toby' Grantham

Sailor (Trafalgar)	
'Trafalgar'	At the back of a sea chest with a medallion of Nelson's Flagship 'Victory'
Lord Howe	
'Lord Hou'	
Rodney	
'make the fiddler drink for why with fiddling he is dry'	inscribed on coat
J Marsh Jolley	on base
John Bull	
'Account'	on paper held in hand

Chapter Eight
Twentieth Century Toby Jugs

The history of Toby Jugs after 1900 has followed a similar pattern to that of the earlier period. Once again we have a few Tobies of high quality and many of a poorer quality. There are still problems of identifying makers but thankfully these are confined to the poorer end of the range of Tobies produced in the 1930s and 40s. The 'Ordinary' Toby as well as several other Toby characters continued to be produced after 1900, some of these as clever fakes of the original and others as more honest representations of popular designs. Many of them have proved to be very desirable and are much sought after by collectors.

It was in the 1920s and 30s that the revival of Toby Jugs as a quality production item took place. Thanks to the commercial success of jugs produced by pottery manufacturers such as Doulton and Wilkinson Ltd, there was an upsurge in the production of jugs by other potters. Sadly, as we have come to expect with Toby Jugs, not all of these were up to the standard of Doulton and Wilkinson, but many new variations in size, shape and function were introduced, several of which proved very popular, particularly crested ware, miniatures and character jugs.

The production of other Toby items come under a miscellaneous group which is largely comprised of utility pieces that are in fact converted and contorted versions of the 'Ordinary' Toby. Ranging from teapots and cream jugs to tobacco jars they were no doubt introduced because of the commercial success of Toby Jugs. Apart from those by potters such as Doulton and Beswick they are in the main unmarked and very little is known about them as production records are not available.

The Toby Jug has undergone further development with the introduction of the 'cousin' of the Toby Jug, the character jug. The most notable of this type is that produced by Royal Doulton. A character jug portrays the head and shoulders of its chosen subject as opposed to the full body of a Toby Jug. Whilst to many Toby collectors these represent a travesty of the real thing they are nevertheless extremely popular in their own right.

Throughout this century there has been a great expansion in the characters portrayed by Toby Jugs, from working tradesmen of all sorts to religous characters such as Monks, Friars and Cardinals. Recent history has provided several new characters for British Toby modellers to explore, from Presidents to Admirals.

The most often portrayed figure in Toby from this century is undoubtedly Sir Winston Churchill who was first represented in a Toby form in 1927. This jug by W H Goss proved to be the first of many which portray the man at various stages of his great political career. Other distinguished politicians such as Lloyd George have also been modelled, and recently a limited edition character jug of Ronald Reagan has been produced by Royal Doulton.

The characters of Charles Dickens have proved very popular with Toby producers this century, as have the characters popularised by Shakespeare.

There have even been several individuals who for one reason or another have specifically commissioned Toby Jug likenesses of themselves to be produced. We will look at some of these later.

The appeal of the Toby seems to be unrelenting and the popularity of the Toby Jug is now universal with many foreign makers. The success of the Toby concept can be best illustrated by the number of Tobies now produced overseas which portray the characters of particular countries. A lovely example of this is the Carribbean girl Toby produced in the Virgin Islands. Toby Jugs are now to be found as far afield as Mexico and Japan. The first Japanese Toby Jugs were produced in the 1940s as direct copies of British Toby characters. The USA in particular has many collectible home produced Tobies as well as an established collectors market in British Toby Jugs.

W H Goss, Churchill Toby Jug 1927.
Courtesy N Pine

A Royal Doulton Character Jug: Clark Gable
Courtesy J Lukins

Known 20th Century Toby Makers	Main Production Dates
Avon Ware	1950s
Artone	1960s
Ashtead Potteries	1920s
Arcadian	1940
Barum	1890s
Burlington Ware	1950s
Burgess and Leigh	1940s
Burleigh Ware	1950s
Beswick	1940s
Carlton	1930
Charles Allerton & Sons	1900
C H Brannan Ltd	1900
Copeland Spode	1947
Clarice Cliff	1941
Crown Devon	1940
Chelsea	1950·
Cooperclayton	1940
Denton	1940
Devonmoor	1940
Franklin Porcelain	1978
Gladstone Pottery	1960
Grafton	1940
Keele Street Pottery	1950
Lancaster	1950
Leonard Jarvis	1945
Lord Nelson Pottery	1859
Price of Kensington	1950s
Royal Doulton	1930s
Doulton Burslem	1920s
Royal Winton	1930s
Roy Kirkam Pottery	1970s
Royal Worcester	1920s
Savoy	1930s
Sandland	1930s
Shelley China	1910
Shaw & Copestake Sylvac Staffordshire	1901
J Shaw & Sons	1940s
Shorter and Son	1950
Studio 82	1970s
Thornly	1940s
Thorley	1930s
Wade	1930s
Wain (Melba Ware)	1940s
William Ault	1910
W H Goss	1930s
Wilkinson Ltd	1920s
William Kent Ltd	1900s
Wood & Sons	1900
Willow Art & Willow China	1920s
Wedgewood & Co	1930s

The Major Twentieth Century Potters

Ashtead Potteries

Mainly produced for the American market in the 1920s these Tobies portray a range of historical characters in cream ware such as Lloyd George, Baldwin and Benjamin Franklin. The jugs tend to be of a poor quality but are interesting to collect in view of the history they portray. They are usually reasonably priced at around £50.

A similar group of 'political' jugs may have been produced by Ashtead, probably about 1925. These were; Earl Lloyd George, Sir Harry Lauder, Earl Baldwin, Ramsey Macdonald and Lord Asquith. All of these subjects are seated, 6″ high and well modelled in subdued enamel colours. The only marks on them are raised numerals on the base, about half an inch in size. Macdonald bears the number 452 and Earl Baldwin 451. The potter of these also made a male and a female Toby in the same fashion as the above group. The 'political' jugs are valued at between £50 and £200.

Beswick Tobies and Character Jugs

As a result of the recent growth in interest in Beswick items generally, the Tobies and character jugs are now rising in value and collectability. Produced in the 1930s they are of appeal to Beswick collectors and Toby collectors alike. Values have in recent years been rising but the jugs can still be found for less than £30 in many cases. The two exceptions to this are 'Little Nell's Grandfather' and 'Betsy Trotwood' which are particularly difficult to obtain and are valued at around £60. Many of the characters produced were adopted by Beswick into a range of miscellaneous items such as sugar and cream jars and salt and pepper pots.

Character	Reg. No	Production Dates
Toby Jugs		
Toby Phillpot	1110	1948-1969
Toby Phillpot 6.5″	1111	1948-1969
Midshipman	1112	1948-1969
Martha Gunn	1113	1948-1960
Barrel Toby	1114	1948-1960
Character Jugs		
Tony Wellor	281	1934-1973
Mr Micawber	310	1934-1973
Sairey Gamp	371	1936-1973
Scrooge	372	1936-1973
Old Bill	735	1939-1940

Character Jugs (cont.)

Navy	736	1939-1940
Air Force	737	1939-1940
Winston Churchill	931	1941-1946
Pecksniff	1117	1948-1973
Pickwick	1119	1948-1973
Captain Cuttle	1120	1948-1973
Barnaby Rudge	1121	1048-1969
Mr Vardon	1204	1950-1973
Martin Chuzzlewit	2030	1965-1973
Little Nell's Grandfather	2031	1965-1973
Mr Bumble	2032	1965-1973
Betsy Trotwood	2075	1966-1973
Falstaff	2095	1967-1973
Henry VIII	2099	1967-1973

The Beswick Toby Phillpot in both sizes and the Midshipman.

A group of Beswick Character Jugs.

Burlington Ware

'Burlington ware' was a mark found on the products of J Shaw of Tunstall 1931-1963 who produced a range of relatively inexpensive jugs, particularly in the 1950s. All the jugs are over 6″ in height, some up to 12″, and the characters portrayed include the Sleeper, Singer, Captain Hook, John Bull and Long John Silver.

The Long John Silver is a poorly modelled jug which is really an injustice to one of the greatest characters in British literature. He is, as to be expected, standing on one leg with the aid of a crutch. He wears a long red or green coat, and black tricorn hat with a yellow band around the brim. On his right shoulder is a parrot and in his right hand he holds a cutlass. Around his waist is a belt which has a pistol thrust through it. It is a common jug and can be bought for around £30. The others have a similar value.

Burleigh Tobies

This pottery produced a range of Shakespearian and Dickens characters in the 1950s. These well made jugs range in height from 3″ to 6″ and were mainly produced for export although they are reasonably common in the UK and represent fair value at their present low cost of £10-£20.

Burgess and Leigh

This pottery produced three different jugs portraying Winston Churchill in the 1940s, with different inscriptions:

1 Bulldogs script . . . "We shall defend every village, every town and every city."
2 "John Bull Churchill"
3 Character jug (Blue jacket) as 1.

They are usually to be found for between £40 and £60.

Chelsea

A range of characters in a brown coloured ware have been produced since the 1950s. These unmarked jugs are usually between 8″ and 10″ in height although they can in some cases be as high as 12″.

Copeland Spode

Known to have produced a range of Tobies in 1947 and possibly into the 1950s, the most collectible is the 8½″ Winston Churchill, seated and smoking a cigar. He was decorated in bright blue and yellow colours, although some were issued in all white because between 1945 and 1952

Burgess & Leigh Churchill.

Copeland & Spode Churchill 1941.

no coloured ware was permitted in Britain.

This Toby is not very rare and sells for around £60. A Franklin Rosevelt Toby was also made by Spode.

Crested Wares Tobies

In the 1880s Adolphus Goss, the son of a Stafford pottery manufacturer, came up with the novel idea of producing miniature porcelain items carrying individual town's coats of arms. These were sold as souvenirs to holiday makers. Other manufacturers soon followed and 'crested ware' proved to be very popular. The W H Goss factory moved its total output into this area and entered a sustained period of growth. The objects portrayed seemed to cover every conceivable subject from churches to antiques, but it was not until the 1930s that Toby Jugs were introduced by Goss and other makers in any quantity and range.

Crested Tobies are to be found ranging is size from miniatures at 1½″ to larger versions of 4″. Listed on the next page are those Tobies that were either produced by Goss or by other makers on behalf of Goss. In all cases (apart from the odd female type), 'Ordinary' Tobies were produced.

Other crested ware Tobies which were not produced by Goss are often judged by collectors as being slightly inferior in value, in spite of

W H Goss Stratford on Avon Toby Jug 58mm high. Value £65. This comes with a matching Toby Basin, worth £80. Courtesy of N Pine.

W H Goss Welsh Lady Jug, 94mm £30. Carries impressed Welsh inscription of 'Pour the Cream'. Courtesy of N Pine.

W H Goss, coloured Toby holding pipe, 50mm, value £60.

W H Goss Giant Toby Jug, 160mm bearing the popular rhyme 'No tongue can tell . . .', worth £120.

the fact that, as previously mentioned, many Goss Tobies were produced for Goss on their behalf. Apart from the Stratford Toby and the Churchill, all Goss Toby Jugs were made in the Thirties. Examples can be found varying in size from 1¾″ to 6½″. There are many other additional crested ware examples of Toby Jugs. These are very similar as many makers including Goss used the same manufacturers moulds. These range in size from miniatures at 1¼″ to others as high as 4″ and are to be found in a range of colours.

W. H. Goss Toby Jugs

Stratford On Avon Toby Jug		Value £65
Stratford On Avon Toby Basin		Value £80
Churchill Toby Jug		
"Any Odds-bar one thats me who kiss the Blarney Stone"	6½″	Value £115
	2¾″	Value £60
British Sailor (blue colouring)		Value £45-£60
Miniatures (male and female)	1⅝″	Value £55-£60

'Ordinary' Tobies	Size	Value
White glazed and crested	2¾″	£40-£45
	3¼″	£45-£50
Multi coloured	2⅛″	£55-£60
	2¾″	£55-£60
	3½″	£60-£70
	4″	£90-£100
	4″	£90-£100
	8¾″	£115-£125
	6½″	£110-£120
One Arm Handle Toby	3½″	£60-£70
	6½″	£110-£120
Female Toby	2¾″	£55-£60

Baby W H Goss miniature, only 40mm high yet very detailed, £60

Female Jug by W H Goss, coloured and 70mm high, value £60.

Information courtesy of 'The Price Guide to Goss China' by Nicholas Pine and published by Milestone Publications

Other Crested Ware Toby Jugs

Toby Jugs

The more desirable specimens made by the heraldic china factories in Staffordshire between 1890 and 1940 were the coloured versions not bearing coats of arms. The crested varieties are less expensive and were produced in a multitude of different shapes for the collector. The majority of these delightful porcelain jugs are less than 4 inches high. As well as Toby Jugs, the Staffordshire potteries of the Edwardian era produced an exciting range of character jugs, depicting animals as well as personalities. The crested Toby Jugs are still under-rated and could well prove to be a good investment in the future.

Arcadian

'Ordinary'	2½″	£30-£50
	3⅜″	£30-£50
Sailor (fully coloured with rope handle)	4″	£30-£50
Black boy Toby (fully coloured)	4″	£30-£50

Carlton

'Ordinary' Toby with verse	4½″	£30-£40

Many others to be found up to £20 in value.

Grafton China
(all fully coloured)
Welsh Lady, John Bull, Irishman, Scotsman.
Value £30-£50

Savoy China
This factory has produced a range of fully coloured Toby jugs without any crests on them. They are all about 2″ high.

Willow Art and Willow China
This factory is known to have produced several crested Tobies that are fully coloured, several of which were no doubt produced for Goss. Current values between £5 and £20.

For further information, please refer to "Crested China" by Sandy Andrews and "The Price Guide to Crested China" by Sandy Andrews and Nicholas Pine (Milestone Publications, Murray Road, Horndean, Hants.)

Comical wide coloured Toby Jug by Arcadian china, worth £25.

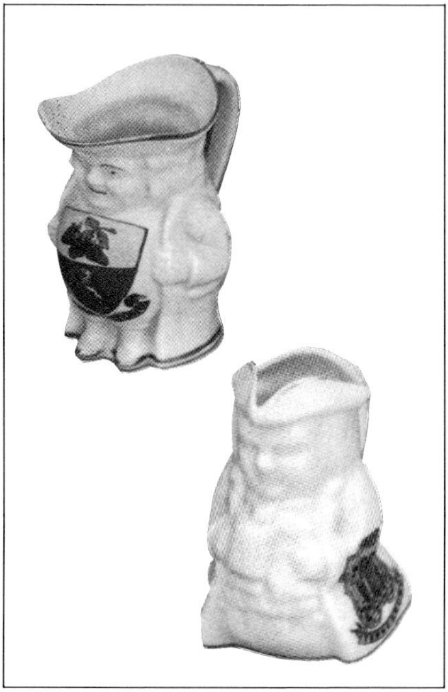

Two jugs by Arcadian and a Willow three-cornered hat example, range £4-£8.

Willow Art, Arcadian, Shelley and Carlton Jugs, range £20 for the Sailor down to £4.

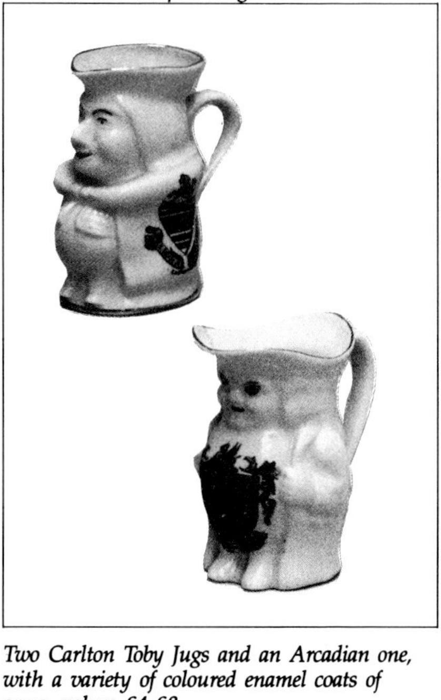

Two Carlton Toby Jugs and an Arcadian one, with a variety of coloured enamel coats of arms, values £4-£8.

Devonmoor

This pottery produced a selection of miniature Tobies below 2″ in height during the 1940s. Their quality is not particularly notable and they are not very collectible. Value £10-£20.

Denton

Their mark is to be found on a range of miniature Dickens characters along with other characters such as Punch. All the jugs are around 3″ in height and are quite collectible although fairly reasonable to purchase. Value £20-£30.

Leonard Jarvis

Winston Churchill

Without doubt this is the finest twentieth century Toby Jug that has been made. Sir Winston Churchill was modelled by Leonard Jarvis and possesses the fine translucent glazes of the Wood-type. Its conception was inspired by Lord Mackintosh and it shows Churchill in his famous 'Victory' pose with the two fingers of his right hand raised. His left hand holds a palette and brushes and at his right foot is a pile of letters with an inkwell and quill pen on top, whilst there is a trowel at his left foot. We thus see Winston Churchill for his many attributes, as war leader, painter, 'brick-layer', and writer.

This Toby is 7″ high and signed 'L. Jarvis'. It was made in a limited edition and it is also numbered, though the limit to the edition is not known. The going price in 1983 was £400 but since then none have appeared on the market. One would expect the price to be considerably higher now.

The Leonard Jarvis Churchill Toby. Courtesy R. Smith.

Lord Mackintosh

This was a one-off modelled by Leonard Jarvis. It is probably still in the possession of Viscountess Mackintosh, the jug being made in Wood-type glazes, similar to the Winston Churchill jug. It shows Viscount Mackintosh of Halifax who took a great interest in the pottery industry and was a major Toby Jug collector. He sits in a chair with his coat of arms emblazoned on the left side of the chair. He is dressed in traditional eighteenth century costume and in his right hand he holds a pottery bust, his left hand carrying what appears to be a pipe.

Royal Winton

Winton are known to have produced a character jug of Winston Churchill in 1941, his famous cigar forming the handle. Other character and Toby jugs may have been produced by this company. Price Range £20 to £30.

Royal Doulton Burslem

Without doubt the most commercially successful Toby Jugs this century have been produced by Royal Doulton. Amongst collectors and dealers many of their withdrawals produce some quite startling prices, the world record price for a Toby Jug being recorded for a Charlie Chaplin which sold for over $7,000 dollars privately in America. However this is 'peanuts' compared to the £15,000 paid for the character jug, 'Toby Gillette' at auction in London in 1984 (as you will see, the character jug is the cousin of the Toby, about which, more later). The company today continues to produce a range of good quality Tobies that are far superior to any other currently produced.

Current Royal Doulton Tobies

Large	**Small**	**Medium**
Falstaff	Happy John	Jolly Toby
Happy John	Honest Measure	Winston Churchill
Hunstman	Falstaff	
Sherlock Holmes	Winston Churchill	
Sir Frances Drake		
Winston Churchill		

Discontinued Royal Doulton Tobies

These jugs were either produced as pilots or were only produced for a short time. Rarity is a far more important factor amongst these jugs than age alone. All of the Doulton Tobies listed below are worth far more than the average Victorian jug, despite being nearly 100 years younger. These jugs are very easy to identify by the Doulton backstamp and the style and quality of the modelling and colours.

Best is not too good	1939-1969	4½″	D6107	£150
The Squire	1950-1969	6″	D6319	£150
Double XX	1939-1969	6½″	D6088	£160
Old Charley	1939-1960	large 8¾″	D6030	£125
		small 5½″	D6069	£115

The Dickens Seated Tobies Set

These were all produced between 1938 and 1960 as part of a range of Dickens decorative items by Royal Doulton. The six seated Tobies are all 4½″ in height and were designed by Harry Fenton. They are very popular amongst Doulton collectors and they regularly sell for between £100 and £130. The set comprises:

Fat Boy	Mr Pickwick
Captain Cuttle	Sainey Gamp
Mr Micawber	Sam Weller

The Dickens Seated Toby Set.

The Kingsware Huntsman. Courtesy J Lukins.

The Charrington Tobies. Courtesy J Lukins.

Charrington Tobies

Produced in 1934 to advertise Charrington ales. Two versions were made, the only difference being in the advertising copy around the white base of the jug. They stand 9½″ in height and a similar number of each is understood to have been produced. Market values £80-£100.

George Robey

This is a very attractive Toby Jug and was produced by commission in 1926. The jug portrays the popular music hall artist George Robey who was known in his time as the Prime Minister of mirth. The jug is 10½″ in height and has a detachable hat as a lid. 'George Robey' is etched on the front of the base.
Market value £3,000-£4,000.

Charlie Chaplin

This is very similar in style to the George Robey Toby and was produced in 1918. It stands just over 11″ high with a detachable bowler as a lid and carries the inscription 'CHARLIE' on its front.
Market Value £3,000-£4,000.

Silver Rim Huntsman

This is a variation of the Kingsware Hunstman jug that was introduced in 1910 at the Burslem studios. It has a distinct silver rim around the top which is hallmarked 1919. It is undoubtedly a pilot piece only one example having been uncovered and this sold at Phillips auctioneers for £200 in 1980, a sum which would be considerably exceeded if it or another were to appear today.

The Cliff Cornell Toby Jug

These jugs were made in 1956 by private commission for the American industrialist Cliff Cornell. His likeness to Churchill and his fascination with the man are borne out by the end product which is very similar to the Toby Jug of Winston Churchill. Cornell specifically requested the similarity in style.

The jugs come in two sizes 9″ and 5½″, and in three colours, brown, blue and tan. The brown and blue version were produced in quantities of 500 each for the large size and 375 for the smaller size. The production run for the tan version is unknown but there seem to be far less, it being difficult to find and the most expensive to buy. The blue and brown versions sell at between £250 and £300 each.

Cliff Cornell Toby with photograph.

Examples of Harry Simeon Pieces. Courtesy J Lukins

DOULTON BURSLEM AND LAMBETH STUDIOS

Although Doulton and Watts had produced a few Toby Jugs in the 19th Century, it was not till the 1920s that Toby Jugs started to become a significant output of the company. These Toby Jugs, produced between 1910 and 1930 are a tribute to the skills of the designer Harry Simeon. The success of all future Doulton Tobies was inspired by the early work of this designer. All of his work portrays stoneware 'Ordinary' type Toby Jugs, others sitting astride stoneware barrels. Many were incorporated at Doulton's Lambeth factory into other objects such as ashtrays, tobacco jars and teapots.

DOULTON CHARACTER JUGS

Through the development work of Charles Noke and Harry Fenton, Royal Doulton launched a range of character jugs after the introduction of John Barleycorn in 1934. After its introduction the series gradually grew in popularity and new characters were introduced over the years. The characters are all chosen from real or fictional people from song, literature, legend or history depicting subjects as diverse as Dick Turpin and the Mad Hatter. The initial introductions were all British characters but recent years have seen the introduction of several American subjects.

As the sales of an individual character jug fell over the years it would be discontinued and another character would be introduced into the series. This was by no means a regular process but by 1985 Royal Doulton had introduced 166 characters, 104 of which have now been discontinued. As some characters were produced in three sizes or more this means that a total of 257 individual jugs have been withdrawn.

These are now without exception worth far more and in some cases staggeringly more than their retail price at issue. There is a huge worldwide market of Royal Doulton character jug collectors and competition between them has forced up prices beyond the current levels of Toby Jugs proper. The company has in recent years introduced a limited edition series of 9,500 which have quickly sold out and immediately risen in value at a constant rate on the discontinued market. Estimates as to the actual number of collectors worldwide vary but it is generally estimated as being well over 10,000 spread across America, Canada, South Africa, New Zealand, Australia and Britain.

RARE DOULTON CHARACTER JUGS

All of the following are for reasons of production exceptionally rare and competition amongst collectors has pushed their market values over £1,000.

Character	**Value**
Red Hair Clown	£1,200 plus
Black Hair Clown	Impossible to estimate
Brown Hair Clown	£1,400 plus
The Cabinetmaker	Impossible to estimate
The Yachtsman (min and small size only)	£1,600 plus
Single Rat Pied Piper	£7,000 plus
Goatee Beard Cavalier	£1,600 plus
Yellow Crown Old King Cole	£3,000 plus
Yellow Crown Old King Cole Musical Jug	£3,000 plus
Clark Gable	£3,500
Hatless Drake	£2,000
White Churchill	£6,500
Kingsware McCallum	£1,200
Blue Pearly Boys	£2,000 plus
Blue Pearly Girls	Impossible to estimate
Miniature Trapper	£800
Miniature Lumberjack	£800
Half Size Jockey	Impossible to estimate
Baseball Player	Impossible to estimate
Buffalo Bill	Impossible to estimate
Maori	Impossible to estimate
Toby Gillette	£15,000

Values when given are courtesy of Kevin Pearson, author of the annual price guide, *The Character Jug Collectors Handbook*.

Ordinary Drake with Hatless version. Courtesy of Christies of South Kensington.

Pearly Girl.

The pilot Buffalo Bill.

Alphabetical Listing of In-Production Character Jugs

Character	Year of Introduction	Large	Small	Miniature	Medium
		Available in			
Annie Oakley	1985	■	■	■	☐
Anthony & Cleopatra	1985	☐	■	■	■
Anne Boleyn	1975	☐	☐	☐	■
Anne of Cleves	1980	☐	■	■	■
Aramis	1956	☐	☐	☐	■
Athos	1956	☐	☐	☐	■
Auld Mac	1938	☐	☐	☐	■
Bacchus	1959	☐	☐	☐	■
Beefeater	1947	☐	☐	☐	■
Benjamin Franklin	1983	■	☐	■	■
Buffalo Bill	1985	■	■	■	☐
Catherine of Aragon	1975	☐	☐	☐	■
Catherine Howard	1978	☐	☐	☐	■
Catherine Parr	1981	☐	■	■	■
Davy Crockett & Santa Ann	1985	☐	■	■	■
D'Artagnan	1983	☐	■	■	■
Don Quixote	1957	☐	☐	☐	■
Doc Holliday	1985	■	■	■	☐
Elvis Presley	1985	☐	■	■	■
The Fireman	1984	☐	☐	☐	■
Falstaff	1950	☐	☐	☐	■
Falconer	1960	☐	☐	☐	■
George Washington	1982	☐	■	■	■
Golfer	1971	☐	■	■	■
George Harrison	1984	■	■	■	☐
Geronimo	1985	■	■	■	☐
Groucho Marx	1984	☐	■	■	■
Hamlet	1982	☐	■	■	■
Henry V	1982	☐	■	■	■
Henry VIII	1975	☐	☐	☐	■
Humphrey Bogart	1985	☐	■	■	■
Jane Seymour	1979	☐	■	■	■
Jimmy Durante (withdrawn in 1985)	1984	☐	■	■	■
John Lennon	1984	■	■	■	☐
Lawyer	1959	☐	☐	☐	■
Long John Silver	1952	☐	☐	☐	■
Louis Armstrong	1984	☐	■	■	■
Lobster Man	1968	☐	☐	☐	■
Monty	1946	☐	■	■	■
Macbeth	1982	☐	■	■	■
Mae West	1982	☐	■	■	■
Mark Twain	1980	☐	☐	■	■
Merlin	1960	☐	☐	☐	■
North American Indian	1967	☐	☐	☐	■
Neptune	1961	☐	☐	☐	■
Old Salt	1961	☐	☐	☐	■
Othello	1982	☐	■	■	■
Paul McCartney	1984	■	■	■	☐
Porthos	1956	☐	☐	☐	■
Poacher	1955	☐	☐	☐	■
Ronald Reagan	1984	☐	■	■	■
Romeo	1983	☐	■	■	■
Ringo Star	1984	■	■	■	☐
Robin Hood (2nd version)	1960	☐	☐	☐	■
Rip Van Winkle	1955	☐	☐	☐	■
Sairey Gamp	1935	☐	☐	☐	■
Sleuth	1973	☐	☐	☐	■
Santa Claus	1984	☐	☐	☐	■
William Shakespeare	1983	☐	■	■	■
Wild Bill Hickock	1985	■	■	■	☐
Wyatt Earp	1985	■	■	■	☐
WC Fields	1983	☐	■	■	■

☐ Sizes available ■ Sizes not available

Alphabetical Listing of Discontinued Character Jugs

Character	*Production Dates*	*Available in* *Large*	*Small*	*Miniature*	*Tiny*	*Intermediate*
'Ard of Earing	1964-67	□	□	□	■	■
'Arriet	1947-60	□	□	□	□	■
'Arry	1947-60	□	□	□	□	■
Apothecary	1963-83	□	□	□	■	■
Auld Mac (Owd version)	1938-45	□	□	■	□	■
Beefeater (GR Handle)	1947-53	□	□	□	■	■
Bootmaker	1963-83	□	□	□	■	■
Blacksmith	1963-83	□	□	□	■	■
Buz Fuz	1948-60	■	□	■	■	□
Captain Ahab	1959-84	□	□	□	■	■
Captain Cuttle	1948-60	■	□	■	■	□
Captain Henry Morgan	1958-81	□	□	□	■	■
Captain Hook	1965-71	□	□	□	■	■
Cardinal	1936-60	□	□	□	□	■
Cavalier	1940-60	□	□	■	■	■
Cavalier (goatee beard version)	1940	□	■	■	■	■
Churchill	1940-42	□	■	■	■	■
Clown Red Hair	1937-42	□	■	■	■	■
Clown White Hair	1951-55	□	■	■	■	■
Custer & Sitting Bull	1984	□	■	■	■	■
Dick Turpin (1st version)	1935-60	□	□	□	■	■
Dick Turpin (2nd version)	1960-80	□	□	□	■	■
Dick Whittington	1953-60	□	■	■	■	■
Drake	1940-60	□	□	■	■	■
Drake (hatless version)	1940	□	■	■	■	■
Farmer John	1938-60	□	□	■	■	■
Fat Boy	1940-60	■	□	□	□	□
Fortune Teller	1954-67	□	□	□	■	■
Friar Tuck	1951-60	□	■	■	■	■
Gardener	1973-80	□	□	□	■	■
Gladiator	1961-67	□	□	□	■	■
Gondolier	1964-69	□	□	■	■	■
Gaoler	1963-83	□	□	□	■	■
Gone Away	1960-81	□	□	□	■	■
Granny	1935-84	□	□	□	■	■
Grant & Lee	1983	□	■	■	■	■
Guardsman	1963-83	□	□	□	■	■
Gunsmith	1963-83	□	□	□	■	■
Gulliver	1962-67	□	□	□	■	■
Izaac Walton	1952-82	□	□	■	■	■
Jarge	1950-60	□	□	■	■	■
Jester	1936-60	■	□	■	■	■
Jockey	1971-75	□	■	■	■	■
John Barleycorn	1934-60	□	□	□	■	■
John Doulton	1984	■	□	■	■	■
John Peel	1936-60	□	□	□	■	■
Johnny Appleseed	1953-69	□	■	■	■	■
Lord Nelson	1952-69	□	■	■	■	■
Lumberjack	1967-82	□	□	P	■	■
Mae West (American Express Edition)	1982	□	■	■	■	■

Character	*Production Dates*	*Large*	*Small*	*Available in Miniature*	*Tiny*	*Intermediate*
Mad Hatter	1965-83	□	□	□	□	■
Mephistopheles	1937-48	□	□	■	■	■
Mikado	1959-69	□	□	□	■	■
Mine Host	1958-81	□	□	□	■	■
Monty (colour change)	1946-54	□	■	■	■	■
Mr Micawber	1940-60	■	□	□	□	□
Pickwick	1940-60	□	□	□	□	□
Mr Quaker	1985	□	■	■	■	■
Night Watchman	1963-83	□	□	□	■	■
Old Charley	1934-84	□	□	□	□	■
Old King Cole	1939-60	□	□	■	■	■
Old King Cole (yellow version)	1937	□	□	■	■	■
Paddy	1937-60	□	□	□	□	■
Parson Brown	1935-60	□	□	■	■	■
Pearly Boy Brown	1947	□	□	□	■	■
Pearly Boy Blue	1947	□	□	□	■	■
Pearly Girl Brown	1947	□	□	□	■	■
Pearly Girl Blue	1947	□	□	□	■	■
Pied Piper'	1954-80	□	□	□	■	■
Punch & Judy Man	1964-69	□	□	□	■	■
Robin Hood (1st version)	1947-60	□	□	□	■	■
Robinson Crusoe	1960-82	□	□	□	■	■
Sairey Camp	1940-60	(In current production)			□	■
Samuel Johnson	1950-60	□	□	□	■	■
Sam Weller	1940-60	□	□	□	□	□
Sancho Panza	1957-82	□	□	□	■	■
Santa Claus						
(1981 version Doll Handle)		□	■	■	■	■
(1982 version Reindeer Handle)		□	■	■	■	■
(1983 version Sack of Toys Handle)		□	■	■	■	■
Scaramouche	1962-67	□	□	□	■	■
Simple Simon	1953-60	□	■	■	■	■
Simon the Cellarer	1935-60	□	□	■	■	■
Sir Henry Doulton	1984	■	□	■	■	■
Smuggler	1968-80	□	□	■	■	■
Smuts	1946-48	□	■	■	■	■
St. George	1968-75	□	□	■	■	■
Tam O'Shanter	1973-79	□	□	□	■	■
Toby Philpots	1937-69	□	□	□	■	■
Tony Weller*	1936-60	□	□	□	■	■
Toothless Granny	1935	□	■	■	■	■
Touchstone	1936-60	□	■	■	■	■
Town Crier	1960-73	□	□	□	■	■
Trapper	1967-82	□	□	P	■	■
Ugly Duchess	1965-73	□	□	□	■	■
Uncle Tom Cobbleigh	1952-60	□	■	■	■	■
Vicar of Bray	1936-60	□	■	■	□	■
Viking	1959-75	□	□	□	■	■
Veteran Motorist	1973-83	□	□	□	■	■
Walrus & Carpenter	1965-79	□	□	□	■	■
Yachtsman	1971-79	□	P	P	■	■

* Extra large sizes available
□ Sizes available
■ Sizes not available
P Pilot issued

Roy Kirkam Pottery

A modern range of Tobies produced since the 1970s ranging in height from 5″ to 7″. There is very little secondary market activity in these particular jugs and they can usually be found for under £10.

Royal Worcester

This factory produced a small range of coloured Toby Jugs in the 1920s. Those jugs known are listed below although there are believed to be others.

1 Punch and Judy	2″	1920s
2 Mephistophelies	7″	1927
3 Ordinary with cover	6″	1927
4 Ordinary without cover	6″	1927
5 Ordinary with cover	3½″	1927

A small pair of Toby salt and pepper pots were also made in this period.

The value of these particular jugs is related to the desirability of Royal Worcester rather than their appeal as Toby Jugs. They are quite rare and prices have been recorded from £75 to £150.

Sandland

These jugs sometimes marked 'Lancaster' portray an array of characters from Uncle Tom Cobbleigh to Robin Hood. They come in four sizes; tiny, miniature and small with the larger size often found with a silver rim around the handle. All the jugs were discontinued in 1968 and are worth anywhere from £8 to £25 without a silver rim.

Shaw & Copestake Sylvac Staffordshire

At least three variations of small multi-coloured Tobies have been produced at this pottery. They sell for around £20-£30 each.

Shelley

The Shelley pottery have produced five different Toby Jugs at their Foley works at the turn of the nineteenth century, ranging in height from 4″ to 8″. The first three were produced in 1899 in whiteware and multicolouring. The remaining two Toby Jugs were made in 1911 as part of the Intarsio range. Standing 8″ high they are characterised by their dark brown and green colouring.

Since they are collected by Shelley enthusiasts as compared to Toby collectors their values are correspondingly far higher than they

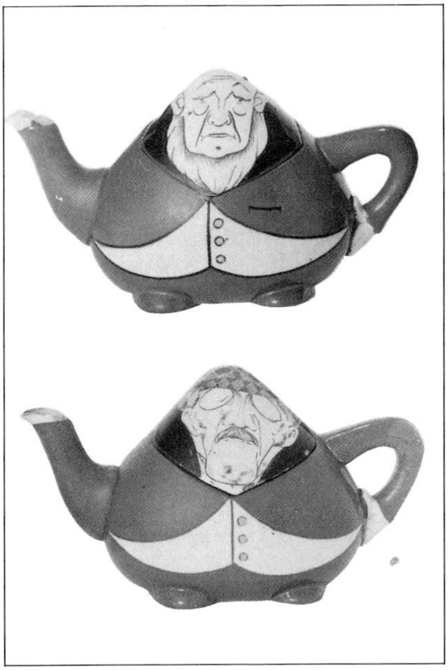

A Foley 'Intarsio' Character Teapot of the South African statesman Kruger and another of a person unknown. They made £450 and £650 respectively at Phillips (London) on 12th Dec 1985.

A Foley 'Intarsio' Toby Jug of Friar Tuck. £260 at Phillips (London) on 13th June 1985.

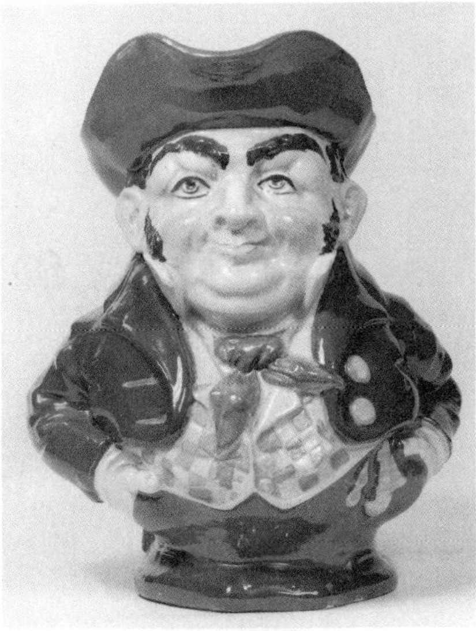

A Foley 'Intarsio' Toby Jug of John Bull. £160 at Phillips (London) on 15th May 1986.

A late Foley Toby Jug of a Victorian Child. £200 at Phillips (London) on 15th May 1986.

might be, being collected in line with other Shelley Ware. The Friar Tuck illustrated here made £260 plus commission at the Phillips auctioneer's Art Nouveau Decorative Arts & Studio Ceramics sale held on 13 June 1985. A similar value can be placed on the other four Shelley Tobies.

Of interest to the collector of miscellaneous Tobies are the Shelley Character Teapots. One will however need a good bank balance as these teapots are very valuable. Made during 1900 they feature ordinary characters as well as several politicians including Lord Salisbury, Gladstone, Chamberlain and the South African politician, Kruger. The modeller for all the teapots was Frederick Rhead. Some characters are found in a taller body as compared to the small body teapots. The value of these items has been increasingly rising with an auction price range of £200 to £650 given by the leading auction house in this area of collecting, Phillips of London.

Shorter & Son

Shorter & Son are known for their character jug of Winston Churchill produced in the 1940s, which has its handle in the form of an anchor. They also produced a range of 6″ Tobies in the 1950s which are quite desirable, many of which are characters that were introduced as character jugs by Royal Doulton, such as Uncle Tom Cobbleigh and Dick Whittington. Market values tend to be on the low side.

See also the 'Ordinary Toby' Chapter 3.

Wade

This factory is known to have produced a character jug for the McCullan company in three sizes, large small and miniature. The large size is identical to that made by Royal Doulton around the same period. They are however only worth a fraction of the Doulton value and can be found for less than £40. See photograph on page 139.

Wain (Melba Ware)

Wain produced a range of characters designed to compete with those produced by Royal Doulton. Although of a high quality they were withdrawn a few years after being introduced in the 1950s as they did not prove a commercial success. They range in size from 7½″ to 12″ high. These jugs are not common but are still quite cheap at around £30 to £40 each.

Wedgwood

The only record of a Toby Jug produced by Wedgwood this century is known as the Elihu Yale Toby. This was produced for the Yale publishing association as part of its series of Wedgwood Yale Tableware in 1933. There were four colours, light brown, plain cream, blue, and dark brown. The Toby was made in an unknown quantity and offered for sale at $4 each or 12 for $39. Highly prized and valued they are not known to turn up in the UK but undoubtedly a few will have found their way back in the hands of Toby appreciators, one being sold in 1985 for £80.

The jug was modelled by Professor Robert G Eberherd from a portrait of Elihu Yale painted in 1717 and owned by the Yale College since a bequest in 1789.

Wilkinson Ltd

Carruthers Gould Jugs

There is little doubt that the finest and most sensational group of potted Tobies in the twenieth century were the eleven jugs modelled

Marshall Foch; King George V; President Wilson; Admiral Jellicoe; Admiral Beatty; General Botha; Winston Churchill; Lord Kitchener; Lord French; Field Marshall Haig; Lloyd George; Marshall Joffre; Old Bill; Jellicoe Character Jug; Kitchener Character Jug. Photo courtesy of Britannia Antiques.

as representations of the First World War Allied Commanders. These were designed by Sir F. Carruthers-Gould and potted by Wilkinson Ltd of the Royal Staffordshire Potteries, retailed by Soanne and Smith Ltd of Oxford Street, London W1.

Sir Francis Carruthers Gould (known as 'F.C.G.') was born in 1844 and died in 1920, being one of the most famous political cartoonists of his time, working mainly for *The Westminster Gazette.* Of many obituary notices, not one mentions his design of the eleven Wilkinson jugs, but this is probably the one thing he will be remembered for in the years to come.

There were eleven jugs potted between 1915 and 1919, the first set of six being;

Name	**Entitled**
Admiral Beatty	*Dread Nought*
Field Marshall Haig	*Push and Go*
Admiral Jelhoe	*Hell Fire Jack*
Marshall Joffre	*75mm Ce que joffre*
Lord French	*French Pour Les Francais*
Rt. Hon. D. Lloyd George	*Shellout*

Each of the above were produced in a limited edition of 350, the first two retailing at £2-12-6 each, the others at £2-2-0 each. They now sell for between £300 and £350 each.

The next two issued were;

President Wilson	*Welcome Uncle Sam*
Marshall Foch	*Av Diable Le Kaiser*

These were produced in a limited edition of 500, retailing at £3.30 each and now sell at £250-£325 each.

The remaining three were;

H. M. King George V *Pro Patria*

The King George V Toby was produced in a limited edition of 1,000, but for some reason there are two variations of the jug. Some are fully coloured and others are all white. These retailed at £7.70. The fully coloured version sells for three times the value of the plain white version, c.£700

General Botha *Loyalty*

General Botha was produced as a limited edition of only 250 and is by far the rarest of these jugs to be found. The retail price was £3.30.

Lord Kitchener *Bitter for the Kaiser*

Lord Kitchener was the last of these Tobies to be produced, but the number produced is hard to determine, as is the retail price. These last three Tobies generally sell for between £325-£375.

Clarice Cliff Tobies

It may have occurred to the reader that eleven is a strange number for a 'set' of figures. Winston Churchill may have been intended to make this number up, and it is suggested that he was the intended twelfth figure. The reason for his omission may have been that he fell out of favour over the 'Dardenelles' affair in 1915. He was certainly not a popular figure as Chancellor during Britain's Twenties slump, but he regained favour during and after World War II. As Sir Carruthers Gould was no longer alive at that time, Clarice Cliff was given the design commission. But in spite of these claims it may be erroneous to make the connection because the Clarice Cliff version is at variance with the World War I set (if only slightly) and was of course made to commemorate Churchill's activities in a different war.

Clarice Cliff's model of Winston Churchill bears the phrase, 'May God Defend the Right' on the front of the base. He is holding a warship in his hands and is dressed in naval uniform, sitting on a bulldog. The jug was potted by the Royal Staffordshire Pottery Co of Burslem (Wilkinson Ltd). It is 11½″ high and was issued in 1941. The current value of this jug is around £500-£550.

Clarice Cliff also modelled a Mr Chamberlain c1940, 12″ high with, 'Justice, peace, happiness and truth' on the base. The current value of this jug is around £400-£500.

Wilkinson also commissioned Clarice Cliff to model a Toby Jug of a man sitting holding a jug of beer on his lap. The figure has a black hat, red face, curly hair, blue coat, white trousers with blue stripes and yellow stockings. It is 8″ high and worth over £150.

William Ault

(Tit Bits Toby)

This was made in 1917. It is a standing figure, 9¼″ high. It was commissioned by George Newnes Ltd in 1917 for the *'Tit Bits'* magazine, and was awarded as a prize in what was called 'Dittoes Competitions'. These jugs were made in an overall green enamel. Toby stands holding a grey open book on the cover of which is printed, 'Tit Bits'. Around the base in raised letters is, 'Tit Bits Toby Jug', these jugs were made by William Ault of Swadlincote near Burton-on-Trent, Staffordshire, They are marked on the underside of the base, 'Ault-England', and their value is around £30-£40. See page 139 for potograph.

Peace 1918 Toby

This Toby is similar to the 'Tit Bits' Toby except that the cover has been adapted to read 'Peace 1918', and around the base, on the front is written '1914 Great War 1918'. Value £60-£80.

William Kent (Old Staffordshire)

William Kent started producing figures and ornaments in Burslem from 1878. His original Toby moulds were obtained from William Machin. He went into partnership with John Parr in 1880 till 1894 and then carried on potting alone. After this his sons and then his grandson ran the pottery until 1962 when it was taken over by the Blakeny Art Pottery.

Right through the 20th century up until 1962 the Kent pottery were producing Toby Jugs in over glaze colours in the style of the 19C potters. These were mainly unmarked but in some cases there is the mark; 'OLD STAFFORDSHIRE WARE ENGLAND'. The following models were produced, and apart from the Squire they are not particularly sought after by todays collectors.

Model	Reg No	Market Value
The Ordinary	387	£50
Hearty Good Fellow	373	£50
The Squire	380	£100
Judy	382	£50
Punch	381	£50
Squat	368	£50
Night Watchman		£50
Jolly Miller	370	£50
John Bull	374	£50
Pickwick	391	£50
Toby Teapot	366	£40
Snuff-taker	390	£40
Kneeling Toby	481	£30
Standing Pot Belly	481	£50

Wood Family Jugs

Tony Wood, the last member of the Wood family to be actively engaged in the industry, is a descendant of the famous Wood family of Burslem (eighth generation). By careful photography of original jugs, the Wood Family were able to reproduce, in new moulds, faithful representations of the originals. The potting is a little on the thick side, but other than that the reproduction is very good, and the jugs are becoming collector's items in their own right. Because these jugs were produced in a limited edition, the moulds were destroyed after the required number had been produced, much to the regret of the makers — something that cannot be said of many so called 'limited editions' by other potters.

The limited edition reproduction Tobies are however considered to be among the best Toby Jugs made this century. There are seven in

Tit Bits Toby.

The Wade McCullam

Wood & Sons 1973 limited edition.

Admiral Lord Howe 1974 limited edition of 500, this is the only one fired in a white.

all; Toby Fillpot ('Ordinary'), Martha Gunn, The Squire, Admiral Lord Howe, the Benjamin Toby ('Ordinary' with raised glass), The Sailor, and Hearty Good Fellow (not a Ralph Wood original). Toby Fillpot and Martha Gunn were potted in a limited edition of 1,000 in 1973, the others in a limited editions of only 500, between 1975 and 1981. Most of these jugs appear to have gone to the United States as apart from the first two mentioned they are little encountered in Britain.

Studio 82

The 'Hearty Good Fellow', made by Tony Wood (Studio 82) Ltd., at Fenton, Stoke-on-Trent. This new company was formed by Tony Wood and Elizabeth Capper with the sole objective of continuing the fine tradition of design and manufacture carried out by the Wood family over the past 200 years. They are currently manufacturing a wide range of low priced Toby Jugs.

Chapter Nine

Collecting Toby Jugs

There are still lots of Toby Jugs about but the ones found in 'junk' shops tend to be just that. Apart from the occasional lucky break, you only get what you pay for, and the lucky breaks are few and far between. But hope springs eternal, and we collectors cannot be deterred from spending our time in junk shops and markets, in spite of the odds against us. There will always be a possibility of the great 'find' which justifies such disproportionate efforts.

The following is an extract from R. P. Way's 'Antique Dealer'* about his efforts to obtain a very nice Toby Jug just before the First World War. He had just sent some 'Ralph Wood' figures to Captain Price, whom he knew to be an avid collector of Toby Jugs:

". . . A friend of mine in Bath asked me whether I would know a Ralph Wood Toby Jug if I saw one. I said I hoped so and he asked me to go with him to Swanage in Dorset. He told me to dress up as smartly as I could, because he had an idea that he would explain to me later. I was extremely puzzled, but I met him the next Saturday at the station wearing my best clothes, yellow wash-leather gloves and a swinging Malacca cane with a silver top.

In the train he explained that the jug belonged to a sullen, bad-tempered innkeeper. The inn was a small one in an out-of-the-way part of Swanage. He knew the man didn't want to part with the jug, but he thought that if I came on the scene, as a rich looking type with money, and if the jug was a good one, I might impress the innkeeper into making a deal.

We got to the inn between five and six o'clock and ordered drinks. My friend took the landlord aside and explained to him what an important customer I was and then he asked him to have a drink with us.

The drinks turned out to be several rounds and then the landlord was asked if he would mind showing me his old jug. Mellowed by what he had taken the landlord said, "Certainly, but 'e ain't for sale mind, 'es willed away 'e is."

When I saw the jug I knew at once that it was a very fine example of Ralph Wood's work, brilliant, absolutely perfect and it

*The passage is reproduced courtesy of Michael Joseph. Every effort has been made to contact the author and his family, but this has not been possible.

even had its original cover, on which R.K. Price was so keen. The face was aubergine, the coat a rich blue and breeches deep yellow. It was a beauty.

While I examined it the landlord rambled on " . . .an' would you believe it, guv'nor, I bin offered £10 for that old jug, daft, ain't it?"

He looked to see if I believed him, but I shrugged and said, "That's nothing — I'll give you double for it."

"Ah, maybe," he retorted sceptically, "it's easy to say things."

"But I mean it, I've the money here." I then started to count out coins from my sovereign purse. As he saw the gold spreading in a small heap on the table, his eyes goggled and he left us say, "I must fetch my old woman."

When he'd gone my friend said, "Quick, spread it all out, I think we may make a fair deal after all." As he spoke, he swivelled round a movable hanging gas jet so that its light shone directly upon the spread-out gold coins.

We were ready by the time the landlord came back with an untidy old woman with red-rimmed eyes. She looked first at us, then at the jug, and lastly at the gleaming golden sovereigns. As she looked her husband muttered to her, "I could buy a pony." Still she stared, then she spoke suddenly, "Oh please yourself," and left the room without another word.

The landlord said, "Well, throw another 'alf quid for luck guv'nor, and the old jug's yours.'

Quickly I threw down another half-sovereign and then, picking up the jug, started to wrap it in the newspaper we had with us.

The landlord shouted excitedly, "Aaf a mo', the boys must see this or they'll never believe me." He rushed to the door and shouted down the passage, "Hey, boys, come up here." Almost at once six or eight rough-looking men stood at the door. For a second I wondered whether we were going to lose both jug and money! But the innkeeper said dramatically, "Boys, I've bin 'an sold me old jug . . ." A long pause and then a roar, "An' THERE'S THE BLOODY MONEY!"

I've never forgotten the vivid scene even after all these years. We, the two dealers with our backs to a small shuttered window, the round table covered with dirty red table-cloth and the beautiful jug surrounded by twenty sovereigns and one half-sovereign in gold. The swarthy, black moustached landlord, his cheeks red with excitement, his eyes gleaming, one hand resting on his hip, the other pointing at the table. The peering, unshaven faces at the door, the smell of beer, sawdust and wafts of shag tobacco, the

atmosphere of avarice and high drama. It was almost an anti-climax to sell the jug afterwards to Captain Price for £95, although we were delighted."

Part of the fun of collecting is 'the hunt'. There can be few millionaire collectors, but it cannot be much fun giving a blank cheque to a top dealer with orders to purchase twenty of the best Tobies. He may end up with one of the finest collections in the land, but it is a bit like giving the fox hunters the dead fox and telling them not to bother with the hunt! Toby hunting is fortunately much more humane. It is often more fun to travel hopefully than to arrive, and my favourite Toby Jug is usually the one that I have just bought, with the excitement of finding it fresh in my mind.

New collectors must read all that they can do on the subject, visit museums and meet and talk to kindred collectors and dealers to build up a knowledge of the subject — there are always new stories, new ideas and new information. It is a good idea to build up a photographic album or a folder using articles from magazines, newspapers and auction catalogues.

It is something of a mistake to start collecting by buying a number of low priced jugs. It is far better to save and buy one good jug than plunge into a cheap collection, for if you buy wisely you will not regret it, you will enjoy the company of your Toby. If you should wish to sell at a later date, you will get your money back with interest. This is not so with the cheap and nasty Tobies, of which there are so many, they do not look particularly attractive and cannot really be resold, so think about this when you purchase.

In the antique ceramics field the usual advice regarding the quality of jugs is "never buy damaged pieces." This may have been true in the past when fine pieces were plentiful and less costly and it is true of modern pieces of fine porcelain, but it is particularly difficult to find Toby Jugs which do not have some element of damage about them. The prices that many damaged jugs fetch can be quite staggering, so don't expect every jug you collect to be perfect and do expect to get good prices even if your jug is damaged.

Restorations

Rarely will one find an early Toby Jug in perfect condition. It will invariably have had to withstand the test of time, which is in some cases over two hundred years. One must therefore be suspicious of an early jug which is in pristine condition.

Staffordshire pottery of the nineteenth century overglaze variety is the easiest to restore. The unsophistication of the pottery lends itself to artificial painting and glazing and this can be done 'cold', although an ordinary household oven can help. The most vulnerable parts of the Toby are the hat (lid and brim) the handle and the small jug in Toby's hand.

The crown or lid of the Toby is often missing from the hat and the reason for this is not difficult to understand — the Toby is often picked up by the unwary and the top comes off, crashing to the ground and breaking — something for collectors to look out for when inspecting a Toby which happens to have its hat. But bear in mind also that the lid may not be the original lid made with the Toby.

It is the fixed brim which most often gets chipped or cracked, and this is where restorations are most likely. There are three ways of detecting this, whether it is restoration to the hat or elsewhere on the Toby. The first is to check whether the crazing on the enamel of the Toby is uniform throughout. Restored areas will not have the crazing of the original. The second test is through ultra-violet light which can reveal the outline of the restoration. Whilst this is a good method, one must beware of taking too seriously a restoration that cannot be detected by the human eye. A third means of detecting a restoration, particularly to the brim, is quite amusing to the on-looker; some hungry looking dealers bite the brim with their teeth in an attempt to find a soft spot or an off sounding vibration, but this is not a method used by the author, in spite of healthy teeth.

The handle is also often restored. It is not uncommon for the handle of an early jug to have come loose from the body, in which case the handle needs to be secured to its former position or replaced. One would obviously prefer the original handle, particularly if it is unusual, so this is something which the collector must also look out for.

The jug in Toby's hand is also a part of the Toby which can be replaced. For some reason the jugs on the early Tobies may have fallen away (probably because they were moulded as a separate item) and what you are looking at may be a substitute for the real thing.

One must remember that in the case of early jugs the detection of a restoration may not alter the value of the Toby. It obviously depends on the extent of the damage which has occurred and the extent to which a seller is trying to 'fake' the quality of his jug.

Other ways of faking jugs, apart from false crazing and 'perfect' restoration, are false dates and marks on the base. Potters themselves are not exempt from this, some late jugs being found with early dates on the front of the base in an obvious attempt to fake the 'real thing'.

Restorations and faking obviously relates to the early jugs rather than the later Victorian ones. Most avid collectors would rather have a damaged Georgian Toby than a pristine Victorian one, so people who cry, "But it's broken" often get the reply, "yes, I know, but have you seen The Venus de Milo?" This remark is of course inapplicable to the experienced collector.

Museums where Toby Jugs can be seen

Victoria and Albert Museum	South Kensington, London
British Museum	Great Russell Street, London
Maritime Museum	Greenwich, London
Brighton Museum	Brighton, Sussex
Nottingham Castle Museum	Nottingham
National Museum of Wales	Cardiff
Royal Scottish Museum	Edinburgh
Yorkshire Museum	York
Stoke-on-Trent City Museum	Hanley
Hull City Museum (The Earle Collection)	Hull
Salisbury Museum	Salisbury, Wilts
Ashmolean Museum	Oxford

Charlie Chaplin by Royal Doulton 1918, the most valuable of all Tobies produced this century.

Bibliography

Astbury, Wheildon, Ralph Wood Figures and Toby Jugs (1922), Captain R K Price

Old English Toby Jugs (1949) Charles Platten Woodhouse FRSA

Toby Jugs (1968) John Bedford

Good Sir Toby (1955) Desmond Eyles

Character Jugs and Toby Jugs (1979) Desmond Eyles

The Mackintosh Collection of Fine Toby Jugs (May 1967) Sotheby & Co Auction Catalogue

English and Scottish Earthenware 1660-1860 (after 1958) G. Bernard Hughes

Staffordshire Chimney Ornaments (1955) Reginald Haggar

A Collector's Guide to Staffordshire Pottery Figures (1971) H. A. B. Turner

The Earle Collection of Early Staffordshire Pottery (1915) Cyril Earle

Jugs (1976) James Paton

The Wood Family of Burslem (1912) Frank Falkner

Collecting Antiques: Georgian Toby Jugs (1949) G Bernard Hughes

Pratt Ware (1984) John & Griselda Lewis

Toby Jugs (Vol II of Connoiseur Concise Encyclopedia of Antiques 1959) Lord Mackintosh of Halifax

Staffordshire Pottery, The Tribal Art of England (1981) Anthony Oliver

The Antique Collectors Club Journal (May 1971)

Toby Jugs (in Antiques Journal–USA May 1947) Edward Wenham

Perhaps Bennington (Antiques Journal–USA April 1950) Gregor Norman Wilcox

Collecting Tobies (The Antique Trader Weekly–USA June 1978) William N McIntyre

Toby Fillpot and his Relations (Apollo c1955) Reginal G Haggar

An Impartial Look at Toby Jugs (in Antique Dealers and Collectors Guide Dec 1984) Anton Gabszewica

The Toby Jug — an Eighteenth Century Grotesque (The Connoisseur March 1904) D. C. Calthorp

Toby Jugs or Fillpots (The Antique Dealer and Collector's Guide April 1947) G. B. Hughes

Ralph Wood and His Contemporaries (Apollo April 1949) S. W. Fisher

Lure of the Toby Jug (The Antique Dealer and Collector's Guide Dec 1954) Arthur Grant

Toby Jugs (Country Life Dec 3 1959) G. B. Hughes

The Fun of Toby Jugs (The Connoisseur June 1954) Lord Mackintosh of Halifax

The Curious Tale of the Toby Jug G. B. Hughes

Toby Jugs are so English (Art and Antiques Oct 1971) Ronald Ellis and Barbara Pearce

A Toast to Toby Fillpot (Art and Antiques April 1975) C. G. L. DuCann

Toby Jugs — The Typical Englishman (The Woman's Journal 1984) Bevis Hiller

A Toast to Toby Jugs (The Antique Trader–USA Feb 27 1985) Morton B Tobias

The British Toby (Collector's World Jan 1986) Francis Salmon

Toby Jugs — The Female of the Species (Collector's World Aug 1985) Vic Schuler

The Toby Jug (The Royal Doulton International Collector's Club Magazine Winter 1985) Kevin Pearson

The Wood Family *Ceramics III* (1986) Pat Halfpenny

See also:
Sir Harold Mackintosh

Antique Collector (March/April 1946)

Apollo (Feb 1939)

Connoisseur (June 1954)

Frank Stoner

Antique Dealer (Feb 1936

G. B. Hughes

Country Life (Oct 1953)

MITCHELLS

Notes